D1580366

A∪

TIT!

ACCESS

Regenerating the Curriculum

Routledge Education Books

Advisory editor: John Eggleston
Professor of Education
University of Keele

Regenerating the Curriculum

Maurice Holt

Routledge & Kegan Paul
London, Boston and Henley

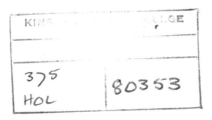
First published in 1979
by Routledge & Kegan Paul Ltd
39 Store Street, London WC1E 7DD,
Broadway House, Newtown Road,
Henley-on-Thames, Oxon RG9 1EN and
9 Park Street, Boston, Mass. 02108, USA
Set by Hope Services, Abingdon
and printed in Great Britain by
Lowe & Brydone Ltd

British Library Cataloguing in Publication Data

Holt, Maurice
Regenerating the Curriculum. — (Routledge education books).

1. Curriculum planning
I. Title
375'.001   LB1570   79-40461

ISBN 0 7100 0300 5

Contents

Acknowledgments

This book is about putting ideas into practice, and draws on the thoughts and experience of many people as well as my own. I owe a debt to the many teachers and others who, in meetings and discussions, have thrown light on aspects of school-based curriculum change.

I am grateful to Colin Bayne-Jardine for his interest and encouragement, and to Nigel Robbins for several helpful suggestions.

My particular thanks go to Professor Denis Lawton, Deputy Director of the London University Institute of Education, and to Philip Waterhouse, Director of the Avon Resources for Learning Development Unit. They were kind enough to read the manuscript and make many valuable comments.

Chapter 1

The Direction of Change

The truth about curriculum change is that it is one thing to talk about it, and quite another to put it into practice and keep it going. The assumption behind the major curriculum development projects of the 1960s was that a central innovating team could devise new approaches and materials appealing enough to be taken up by schools, and acceptable enough to flourish in them. But it was clear by the early 1970s that this was to ask too much of the centre-periphery model of curriculum innovation; putting theory into practice just isn't that easy. Behind any strategy for curriculum change lie assumptions about the nature both of theory and of practice, and unless these ring true the strategy will founder.

My intention is to examine patterns of curriculum change in secondary education, in order to see what can be learnt from the initiatives of the last decade or so, and from the view we have at present of theoretical aims and desirable practical outcomes. The hope is that with a better understanding of what is entailed by the process of curriculum change, we should stand a better chance of implementing it.

Regeneration and the school

To see the task as one of regenerating the curriculum is to imply purpose, plan and engagement. A response is made to perceived influences − the stage, in Popper's original phrase, of situational analysis. Then a process of deliberation leads to an agreed design, and implementing and improving it become a continuous, institutionalised activity. The notion of regeneration certainly rules out haphazard change, as a consequence of passing fashion or secular interest; but it need not imply a utopian stance. The suggestion is of some sort of design — not necessarily a grand one — but one which takes a holistic and not a fragmented view. It may be that some kind of piecemeal change is advocated, and this may be the only possible strategy. But it is difficult not to share the reservations Lawton (1970) has expressed about such approaches:

> Piecemeal reform almost inevitably results in fragmentation of the curriculum, whereas the indications are that what is really required in English schools in the 1970s is far-sighted, long-term planning which would give the curriculum some kind of logical structure and unity.

I have argued elsewhere (Holt, 1978) that while long-term planning of this kind is still largely absent from the curriculum scene, we can at least determine what such a logical structure would look like in a comprehensive school. I have referred to a specific example of which I have direct experience, and indicated in detail the way in which such a structure could be formulated, and its implications for staff, pupils and parents. My chief concern then was with what should be done, and why; my concern now is essentially with how. We must recognise, of course, that what you do is a determinant of how you do it; it is a fundamental error to suppose that the separate aspects of curriculum design, development and evaluation do not form a unity of thought and action. But the complexity of the process warrants different degrees of emphasis, and the emphasis in this book is on what steps need to be taken, by all those agencies involved in the business of education, in order to change schools for the better, and keep them that way.

And this brings us to the central idea of regenerating the curriculum; that it is an activity with the school itself as its focus. It may seem surprising that this should not be taken as self-evident; after all, schools are the places where teachers must make the new ideas work. But almost all our curriculum development so far has been conceived as external to the school. Although the project team would include former or seconded teachers, and its materials would be put on trial in pilot schools, the last people to hear about the new approaches would be the teachers in the user schools themselves. I shall argue that, if we are to regenerate the curriculum, they should be the first people to hear of it.

The subject-based curriculum

In order to develop a perspective on the process of curriculum change, we need to look more closely at how this state of affairs came about. It stemmed, at root, from a view of schooling as the inculcation of prescribed bodies of knowledge, rather than an educative process of initiation into the varied aspects of our culture. The emphasis was on finite ends and well-bounded subjects rather than on developing the pupil's understanding of a complex, inter-connected whole. It was a view based on what Skilbeck (1975) has called 'the traditional static components of "content" and "method"' rather than 'the dynamic fields of relationships, institutional contexts and policy'. In England and Wales, the grammar school was the prime instrument for implementing it; these schools' preoccupation with content comes over clearly from the attempt of Davis (1967) to justify them:

> Amid the clatter of classic and scientist, battle-locked to no great purpose, other subjects with unexceptionable claims and no pretensions to monopoly had been unobtrusively establishing themselves . . . the alternative we are now seeing is a widening of the field of choice to suit a variety of intellects . . . The effect on the grammar schools in terms of sheer volume of study alone is all too familiar.

The grammar school had been established as the official form of English secondary education by the Balfour Act of 1902. In implementing the Act, the Permanent Secretary to the Board of Education, Robert Morant, ensured that the new schools should follow the pattern of the Victorian public schools which, on their home ground of the classics, could offer able pupils from Matthew Arnold to P. G. Wodehouse an education of no direct use but of great strength and

3

sensitivity. But it could be broadened to meet pressure from commercial and cultural influences only by tacking on science, history, languages and so on as extra or alternative subjects, and the new grammar schools lacked the organic coherence that came from residential pupils in the care of powerful housemasters. The introduction of the School Certificate Examination in 1917 confirmed the place of the subject as the basic unit of curriculum structure, and by the 1950s, competition for university entry had led to premature specialisation and, in many of Morant's grammar schools, the shadow of learning but little real substance: except for those in the sixth form lucky enough to sit at the feet of a dedicated teacher and able scholar. The quality of the education offered was a function of individual teachers and subject boundaries rather than curriculum planning and cultural unity.

These schools served the top 20 per cent of the ability range. The remainder (apart from the educationally sub-normal) were to be found after 1944 in the secondary modern schools, which evolved from the old elementary schools and the need to give the lower social orders a grounding in the basic skills needed for the reliable citizen and competent worker. It is an interesting irony that, just as the grammar schools regressed from the noblest ideals of their public school progenitors, so the modern schools bade fair, at one time, to transcend their humbler origins and put the education of the whole child at the centre of their scheme of things. As the Ministry of Education Pamphlet *The New Secondary Education* (1947) put it, the essence of the modern school was 'freedom and flexibility . . . and indeed its great opportunity'. But behind the rhetoric lay the reality of working-class schools that could never aspire to the high-status knowledge purveyed by the grammar schools. The best they could do was to seek credibility by entering their pupils for the same external examinations, and educationally this was perhaps the worst they could do. The insincerity of the whole bipartite system has been neatly summarised by Warnock (1977):

> It seems now to be the height of disingenuousness to combine the theory of competition . . . with the theory that everyone is going to be provided with something

according to his need . . . That if you did not win a grammar school place then . . . you could not have used it with advantage.

The same objection would, of course, apply to any scheme which would allow selective schools to co-exist with comprehensives; it is surprising that some politicians have such short memories.

The position, then, by the beginning of the 1960s was that comprehensive schools were being assembled from components originating from two conflicting traditions; that of the grammar school with its emphasis on external validation in terms of university success, and that of the modern school with its interest in child-centred activities and project-based curricula, alongside the need to justify itself in the examination market-place. This has led, as Lawton (1977a) remarks, to much confusion:

> Today, therefore, we have comprehensive schools without an established tradition either of curriculum or organisation, and without staff trained to plan a curriculum from basic principles. What has happened in most schools is that aspects of the old secondary grammar school curriculum of education for leadership and high status have been mixed up with certain aspects of the old elementary curriculum of basic skills and training for obedience, and the result is often an incoherent mess.

But what we need to notice, for our present argument, is that these two contributory systems have in common – whatever their considerable differences – a knowledge-bound view of schooling in separate subject compartments. And support for schemes to bring them together under one roof came not from any underlying curriculum rationale, but rather from dissatisfaction with 11-plus selection which was already evident by the late 1940s. It was a change in schooling rather than in education. Thus, for example, references to curriculum in Pedley's influential 1964 book on comprehensive schools tell us that 'the subject combinations are flexible', that 'we must stop forcing children to choose one subject to the exclusion of another', and that streaming 'is often in broad blocks rather than finely differentiating one class from another.' Curriculum is a matter of subjects and pupil grouping, and curriculum change is secondary to the task of constructing the new institutions. The jacket description makes it clear on what a slender basis the rationale of the new schools actually rests:

> Nearly everyone interested in education today wants to abolish the 11+ examination, but few people are clear what the alternatives are. The best alternative is some form of comprehensive school . . . .

Curriculum reform and teacher autonomy

To parents, comprehensive reorganisation was a way of avoiding premature selection. To teachers, it was a matter of fitting one subject-based curriculum alongside another, and papering over the cracks by setting and streaming in the 11—14 end of the school, and by option schemes for the 14—16 year olds. The 1960s saw both increasing support for comprehensive schools, and the start of the curriculum reform movement; but this movement had quite different roots, and so had only a glancing effect on the unfolding pattern of reorganisation. It had started across the Atlantic, in the aftermath of the first Russian Sputnik and growing American disenchantment with secondary education which was seen as valuing social skills above academic disciplines. University academics were quick to exploit this unease and the funds that became available for new curriculum projects. This 'academic expertise' style of curriculum development was evident in the Physical Science Study Committee project of 1957, and news of this and similar projects caused the stirrings among English science teachers which led to the first Nuffield Foundation Project — in O-level physics — in 1962. But British practice was to follow subsequently its own path, and it was energised by underlying social and cultural changes which first became evident in Britain in the second half of the 1950s. They had nothing to do with the American feeling of technological inferiority, and everything to do with a sense of release after a dark age of austerity. Booker (1969) has put it thus:

Out of this comparative placidity, however, at the end of 1955 Britain suddenly entered on a period of upheaval . . . the coming of commercial television, the rise of the Angry Young Men, the Suez crisis, the coming of the rock 'n'roll craze . . . When it was over, Britain was a changed country . . . a new spirit was unleashed . . . a pronounced shift of focus from the past to a sense that society was being rapidly carried forward into some nebulously 'modernistic' future.

The emphasis was on newness: Booker has called it the age of 'neophilia', and regards 1964 and 1965 as its most characteristic years. It is interesting to note that one saw the establishment of the Schools Council, and the other, Crosland's Circular 10/65 linking comprehensive schools to DES policy. From the start of the decade, increasing affluence had led to greater choice; the consumer came to expect several products competing for his attention. With newness came built-in obsolescence; the latest record or motor car need be little different from the last. What mattered was only its novelty.

It was inevitable, therefore, that when the tide of change flowed into school staffrooms, it brought to the surface a pattern of curriculum renewal based without exception on the need to up-date subject content. Curriculum was an activity based on separate subjects; refurbishing it for the new age was a matter of taking each in turn, identifying what seemed new and good, and making room for it by eliminating what looked old and tired. Thus were launched the Nuffield Science Projects, the School Mathematics Project, and finally a procession of Schools Council Projects. It is significant, too, that both Nuffield and SMP were launched initially as GCE O-level courses; this was (and still is) the hard currency against which curriculum change can be validated. The eventual linking of CSE to O-level via CSE grade 1 was an acknowledgment that internally-assessed curricula had to be put, as it were, on the gold standard. In the same way, the launching by the Schools Council of projects aimed at only a part of the ability range acknowledged the existence of separate curricula for separate groups of pupils within the comprehensive school.

In the nature of things, up-dating the product means that

a central group has to determine the new message, and then carry the word to the market-place. The approach, as Skilbeck (1975) points out

> is derived from diverse non-educational fields of practical application such as agriculture, engineering and drug production. It is a central part of the industrialized society's need to produce, advertise and sell. It has the unfortunate characteristics of treating teachers and pupils as objects in need of manipulation or redirection . . . of tending to disregard the complex, inter-personal context of teaching . . . .

It is generally known as the research-development-diffusion, or RDD, model of curriculum innovation, following a useful typology of Havelock (1971). It has been the dominant form throughout the British cycle of curriculum development which finally petered out in the aftermath of the 1974 oil crisis. It lends itself particularly well to innovation with a finite end-point; where the output is a product rather than a process. This suited the British emphasis on up-dating content, and in North America it suited curriculum developers who specified, as the measure of their success, the achievement of behavioural objectives. In both cases, the underlying assumption is that the way teachers organise the learning is less important than reaching some goal external to the learning process. It is not surprising, therefore, that the phenomenon of 'tissue rejection' is a frequent consequence of RDD projecteering, once the project team have packed their bags and the school is left to sustain the action.

At first sight, it seems odd that, in a country where the autonomy of the teacher was an influential enough concept to see off by 1964 the Curriculum Study Group of 1962 and determine the shape of the subsequent Schools Council, the principal mechanism for curriculum renewal should be one which put the teacher and the school at the periphery rather than the centre. But as we have seen, the prevailing model of the school was cellular rather than interactive; schooling was simply the sum of subject contributions, and the separate subject was the teacher's fief. It is a view of professionalism closer to that of the plumber than of the doctor or lawyer, where we recognise the importance of specialisms, but tacitly accept that their role is to enrich professional skills rather than limit them. This narrow perception of the teacher's sphere of influence has historical origins. The English seem never to have held education in high regard, and even in the prestigious Victorian public schools, the assistant master was known generally as an usher; the connotation is of child-minder rather than teacher. (There is, indeed, still a private society of public-school masters known as the Ushers' Union.) If, at this time, the status accorded to the teacher could have kept pace with that of the ascending medical and legal professions, the history of our education system might have been very different. But the fact is that until the Education Act 1944, the content of secondary education had been carefully laid down by central government. Whether by accident or design, the Act made no mention of curriculum; and the omission was reinforced in 1950 when the new General Certificate of Education abolished the grouped-subject basis of the old School Certificate. We can see, in short, that not only is teacher autonomy of very recent origin; given the prevailing subject-based system of education at the time when it emerged, it was bound to be interpreted in that same narrow way. It looks inward rather than outward; it looks for boundaries rather than fresh fields.

Given this concept of teacher autonomy, therefore, it smacks of intrusion to see curriculum development as an activity which exploits teacher interactions, and takes the whole curriculum as its territory. The developer is to be not a designer, but a huckster; his task is to bring subjects up to date, and teachers quite properly express their autonomy by examining his wares, and adopting or adapting them if they happen to fit. The basic marketing approach of the RDD model thus made a perfect match with teacher styles in the 1960s, and nowhere was this clearer than in the organisation of the Schools Council, with its teacher majorities at all levels, and underlying structure of purely subject-based committees. Yet the inherent difficulties in holding this line were plainly evident to Maclure (1968), reporting on an international curriculum conference which showed sharp contrasts between British and transatlantic styles:

For Mr Owen [then Joint Secretary of the Schools Council] the teacher was the arbiter of the tolerance of change and was the person who should choose or reject what was offered. For Dr McCarthy [Deputy Minister of Education for Ontario], the teacher could not be knowledgeable about the overall policies or fully comprehend how particular innovation fitted into the whole curriculum . . . When Mr Meade [of the Ford Foundation] said that an effective strategy of curriculum reform demands 'an understanding of the comprehensive nature of change', he pointed to something which the English educational world has been reluctant to recognize. He questioned, by implication, the cosy article of faith that the renewal of the curriculum begins and ends within the school and within a single professional group. In the English context this remains heresy. But whether it can remain so indefinitely as innovation increasingly involves changes which extend beyond single schools to school systems . . . is another matter.

Looking back ten years later, we can identify a number of unfortunate consequences of this style of development. First: however conveniently the RDD model fitted the prevailing *Zeitgeist* and a limited (and limiting) concept of teacher autonomy, teachers do, mercifully, see themselves in practice in more dynamic terms, and will show little enthusiasm for projects that put them at the end of the line. So project take-up has been disappointing, and this represents much wasted effort. Second: to see curriculum development as the up-dating of content may simply ensure, as Skilbeck (1975) puts it, 'a temporary lurch forward followed by a massive consolidation of the status quo. The new materials are regarded as an investment.' They become part of a self-reproducing cycle. Third: the more attention that is devoted to subjects, the less goes to an examination of the whole curriculum. Indeed, the underlying principle is that separate subjects make up the curriculum, and it is no more than the sum of those parts. (Even as late as 1973, a mode 3 proposal for an examination in Design, as an interrelated area, was considered by a CSE panel made up not of a group of teachers who had deliberated on the intricate problems involved in this field, but an *ad hoc* collection of art and craft specialists.) This is not only bad for schools; it is also bad for teachers, because it does not encourage them to look outside themselves and examine broader educational issues. And finally: it is a development that has been bad for the Schools Council. It has seen its task as that of co-ordinating and funding, rather than of examining policy and taking initiatives. And in spite (or perhaps because) of the many interests represented on its vast governing committees, it has not managed to dispel the impression that its curriculum interventions are at once both controlled and limited by the views of teachers' organisations.

But there is a brighter side. Whatever the drawbacks of RDD-style development, it has served to make people aware of the need to examine curriculum assumptions; it has shown the need to spend money on research and development; and it has forged a link, however tenuous, between the world of the classroom and that of the scholar and researcher. Furthermore, the Schools Council's current proposals (1978) to modify its constitution recognise the need to bring a wider influence to bear; to simplify the tortuous committee procedures; to moderate the influence of the subject committees; and − potentially, perhaps the most significant change − to give its secretariat some permanence. Two more points should be made: first, that many of those who have joined in attacking the Council's policies were in a position to modify them during its formative years; and second, it is a unique institution which has attracted some talented staff. Given the prevailing social climate of the 1960s and the political determinants of its structure, it is difficult to see how some of the key decisions could have been otherwise. And when all is said and done, its annual expenditure on curriculum development has never exceeded a million pounds: not much when you consider a system of 30,000 schools, 440,000 teachers, 9 million children and total expenditure in 1978 of more than £7,300m.

Before and after the Green Paper

So it is well to regard hindsight as the privilege of those who view it constructively, and look now at the present climate and its lessons for the future. We must note first the striking change in the spirit of the times. Gone is the insouciant search of the sixties for novelty and effect; gone are the culture of youth, aimless change and an emphasis on the individual at the expense of the institution. Vickers could write, in 1973:

> Although the flood of criticism of institutions has worked much good, it has eroded their authority and thus reduced their power to resolve or contain conflict, which is their main social function.

But by the end of 1976 the mood had changed. Students were no longer revolting; NUS politics no longer extreme. Order was taking the place of randomness. Change, it appeared, was internal and organic rather than external and piecemeal. Two government committees, set up in the days of the *ancien régime*, had failed to adjust to the new climate, and their reports have served only to show us how suddenly everything has changed. First there was the Bullock report on worker participation in industry; and more recently the Taylor report on school governing bodies. Participation, the catchword of the sixties, now has a distinctly dog-eared look; even the erstwhile participators seem to have little stomach for it. It is now more important to make things work effectively than to give everyone a piece of the action.

This, of course, is to paint the contrast in sharper colours than we can readily perceive. But there can be no doubt that we are into a different ball-game, and in education, the new rules can be given a precise date: the Prime Minister's speech at Ruskin College, Oxford on 18 October 1976. This occasion saw the launching of the 'great debate', culminating in the Green Paper *Education in Schools: a Consultative Document* (1977). Politically, this is a document of the first importance. After all, the last explicit government statement on the subjects of the curriculum was the 1935 Regulations for secondary schools. Over forty years had passed since a Minister had dared to trespass into what one of them – Eccles, in 1960 – had termed 'the secret garden'.

There is widespread agreement that Mr Callaghan's intervention showed a nice sense of timing. But to say this is only to acknowledge that the basic cause went deeper than current discontent with comprehensive schooling. The economic crisis of 1974 was a major factor in changing the mood; and we can now see that it represented not a mere hiccup in our own national system, but rather the end of an international era. After twenty years of post-war full employment and increasing affluence, a pattern is unfolding of contracting trade, structural unemployment and tariff protection of national interests. It is a sombre picture, and it is bound to go beyond economic considerations to influence social attitudes. A hard-nosed look at a service which takes 15 per cent of all government spending is scarcely unreasonable; particularly when that represents a 50 per cent increase in real terms on education spending ten years ago. And education had become a first-rate political stalking-horse. The haphazard pattern of curriculum change; the relative ease with which extreme ideas could seemingly infiltrate the system (witnessed, notably, by the affair of William Tyndale Junior School); and chief of all, the failure of the DES or the LEAs to grasp the real nettle of reorganisation, and think about the educational purpose of the comprehensive school: for all these reasons, it was easy to suggest that falling school standards were responsible for rising crime, mounting youth unemployment and stagnating industry.

The great debate, if nothing else, served to show how ill-founded these criticisms were. There is little doubt that standards have risen, and are still rising. The latest national figures show, for example (*Education Statistics, 1975*: HMSO 1978) that whereas in 1967 two out of every five school-leavers managed to get one O-level pass (grade C or above, or its equivalent), the proportion had risen to one in two by 1975. And a study carried out in 1973, published in 1977 (*Comprehensive Education* No. 36) showed that, contrary to popular myth, pupils from working-class backgrounds in well-established comprehensive schools 'achieve greater academic success and get better jobs than they might have expected from a grammar and secondary modern system'. More recently, figures for 1976 and 1977 published by East Sussex Education Authority (*Guardian*, 24.1.78) disclose that 'mature comprehensives in East Sussex are generally outperforming selective schools with similar intakes'.

But while evidence of this kind gives the lie to political fable, it gives no grounds for complacency. It shows rather what excellent things might be done, if the energy and commitment of our teachers could be more effectively directed. Given the effeteness of the grammar schools and the sogginess of the secondary moderns, reorganisation could hardly fail to raise standards. But there are still far too many pupils whose engagement with school is of the sketchiest; only about 20 per cent of our 16-year-olds go on to full-time education, compared with 50 to 90 per cent in other European countries with which we must compete economically. And 40 per cent of our school-leavers went on, in 1975/6, to no education of any kind. This is the real legacy of the old bipartite system, and unless it is replaced by fresh thinking that will enable the comprehensive school to unify its educational experiences as pupils see them, we shall fail to realise its potential.

So let us see how far the Green Paper has got through to the root of the problem. There is no doubt that, in calling for 'a review of curricular arrangements, to be carried out by local education authorities in their own areas in consultation with their teachers', it correctly divines that not even local authorities know in detail how their schools are organised. The important further implication is that it is not enough for teachers to know what schools do; education is a form of individual experience which involves political, moral and cultural issues, and is too important (and expensive) to be left for teachers alone to decide. This is not the secondary issue, of allowing sundry pressure groups to participate; it is the fundamental one of getting schools to take the initiative, and form a partnership with contributory interests which will both enhance the power of the curriculum, and widen the school's influence.

We can also welcome the Paper's clarity about the mishmash programmes served up to so many pupils in comprehensives as a result of the multiple option schemes that have become so widespread:

> the offer of options and the freedom to choose do lead some boys and girls to abandon certain areas of study at an early age . . . it is clear that the time has come to try

to establish generally accepted principles for the composition of the secondary curriculum for all pupils . . .
There is a need to investigate the part which might be
played by a 'protected' or 'core' element of the curriculum
common to all schools.

The paper goes on to recognise that 'the balance and breadth
of each child's course is crucial at all school levels, and this
is especially so during the later years of compulsory education'. The same point is made by HM Inspectorate in the
paper *Gifted Children in Middle and Comprehensive Secondary Schools* (1977):

We agree with the general view expressed in schools that
at least until the age of 16, all pupils, including the gifted,
ought to experience a broad and balanced curriculum
. . . We believe that it is the responsibility of schools to
ensure this balance, and that a pupil should not pursue
his special gifts to the exclusion of other important areas
of the curriculum.

These statements reveal a major shift in DES opinion, and
suggest, too, that the new emphasis finds support in schools.
They encourage us to think that at last, *laissez-faire* planning
– that is, no planning at all – will give way to the coherent,
common curriculum.

How far this will go depends very much on political
factors. Perhaps, in return for fresh favours, the teachers'
organisations might accept the not unreasonable notion of
some centrally determined guidelines for a broad curriculum. But it seems more likely that, at the end of the day, the
familiar but diffident force of osmosis will again be relied
on to diffuse the new doctrine through the schools and the
shires. There is subjective evidence that dissatisfaction with
option schemes is growing in the schools themselves. We
should see, at last, an emphasis in in-service courses on the
key questions which underlie a common curriculum, and we
can be hopeful that the contingent issues that arise in implementing it are competently handled. But how likely is it
that curriculum change will ensue?

The move to a common curriculum

It depends on so many factors: on the head, on the teachers, and on the school's capacity for change; and on all the agencies external to the school which can facilitate change. Subsequent chapters will examine these in turn. But it is incontestable that the pattern of change has now a directed quality about it. The random, what-shall-we-do-next? style of RDD subject-based innovation saddled curriculum development through the 1960s with the aura of a solution looking for a problem. Yet there really was a problem: it was to give coherence to the whole curriculum. By the end of the decade, one or two schools had defined it, and tackled it; but in the nature of things, it is a process of innovation which takes time to mature, and lacks the flashy appeal of instant novelty. Thus new departures like resource-based learning, integrated studies, schools based on participatory democracy and the like attracted a disproportionate degree of publicity, and diverted attention from the whole to the part. New learning strategies, the interrelation of subjects and the delegation of authority are all key aspects of the common curriculum; yet they are peripheral to the real issue, and to elevate any one of them to prime importance is to leave a hole at the centre.

But to see the curriculum as a whole is as much a matter of political as of educational vision, and it is significant that the way ahead has been charted by the Department of Education and Science rather than the Schools Council. Indeed, a striking measure of the extent — and of the speed — of the change in thinking about the secondary curriculum is a comparison of the council's Working Paper 54 on the Whole Curriculum, which appeared in 1975 after four years of deliberation, and the 1977 document *Curriculum 11–16* produced by members of Her Majesty's Inspectorate. While the Schools Council report takes note of 'a widespread feeling that the curriculum should be balanced', it is quick to remind us that many 13-year-old pupils

> have developed firm preferences for some subjects and equally firm antipathies towards others. If they are re-quired to persist with subjects they would rather abandon

they frequently become restless and resentful. Teachers can become dispirited by having to teach such pupils . . . Pupils may legitimately expect to have an effective say in what range of courses they should pursue, particularly in the fourth and fifth years.

But the HMI document asks: 'What do pupils have a right to expect if they are obliged to stay in schools until they are 16?', and concludes that 'there are general goals appropriate for all pupils, which have to be translated into circular objectives in terms of subjects/disciplines/areas of learning activity'. And while the Green Paper finds it difficult to form the words 'common curriculum', and prefers the more evasive 'framework' and 'protected core', the HMIs talk of a common core curriculum, and specify the 'areas of experience' which it should cover: the aesthetic and creative; the ethical; the linguistic; the mathematical; the physical; the scientific; the social and political; and the spiritual. There can be no doubt that in three short years the right problem has been brought to the surface, and that curriculum development here will never be quite the same again.

Our discussion has so far been confined to the position in England and Wales, which are served by the Schools Council. In Scotland, the Scottish Education Department runs The Consultative Committee on the Curriculum, and the usual way of reviewing the curriculum has lately been to set up Working Parties of teachers, school principals, HMI and lecturers from colleges and university education departments. The Munn Report (named after its chairman, and officially titled 'The Structure of the Curriculum in the Third and Fourth years of the Scottish Secondary School') appeared at about the same time as the Green Paper, and faces essentially the same curriculum issues. It handles them with a much surer grasp, avoiding circumlocutions and going beyond the general principle of the common core to suggest how such a programme might take shape. The early part of the report, where the basic criteria for a common curriculum are derived pragmatically but sensibly from both theoretical and practical considerations, is an impressive piece of work that puts the Green Paper quite in the shade. It is the kind of analysis which has been altogether absent from the English scene, and shows how much further our colleagues across the border have gone in working through the implications of a common curriculum. But it will be remembered that Scottish education derived, unlike ours, from a European model; the intense specialisation, for example, of the English sixth form is quite foreign to their approach, and that this has become implicit in their view of 11−16 education has been made clear by Clark (1971), then a member of the Consultative Committee on the Curriculum:

> The aim of the secondary school should be to allow *all* our young people to have full opportunity to . . . receive the best possible *general education* as a preparation for living in our adult society . . . Recognition of the concept of *general education* for *all* and the trend towards acceptance of it at the beginning of this decade might well be considered in the future as one of the major changes in the history of Scottish Education.

This sustained commitment to the view that schools should offer their pupils unifying rather than differentiating experiences is, perhaps, reflected in the less tentative and more closely argued approach of the Munn Report, compared with the Green Paper, to the concept of the common curriculum.

But the important thing is that curriculum change is now unmistakably vectoring in the right direction, and increasingly this influence will be felt in schools. Whether or not national guidelines can be established − and this might be an appropriate task for the reconstituted Schools Council − the view of the Inspectorate will bring a response from local education authorities. I have suggested, too, that this shift in educational opinion is matched by societal influences which, in contrast to the freewheeling sixties, place a greater emphasis on unity and structure.

This kind of mutual reinforcement provides the necessary nerve for tackling the associated political questions of planning and control. The indications are that without interactive currents of this kind, a distinctive pattern of change is unlikely to occur. It is really a matter of acceptability: of the point at which public appraisals merge with theoretical criticism and open up a new path of thought and action. An interesting light on the context of planning decisions has been offered by MacDonald-Ross (1975), who has distinguished between three types of planning:

Normative Planning: Here what *ought* to be achieved is decided according to the prevailing value-system . . . The decision to fight a war, or to shift budgets from tertiary to primary education are essentially normative decisions.

Strategic Planning: Here is determined what *can* be done – given a certain time and situation . . .

Operational Planning: No goal can be obtained if the appropriate sequence of operations is not chosen and put into effect . . . Operational planning is 'instrumental' . . . taking action to attain the goals.

If operational decisions come first, rather than last, in curriculum planning – as, for example, in a *fait accompli* move to abolish streaming, without thought for contingent questions of aims and learning styles – then the process is trivialised and may well be harmful. There is little more to be said for the purely strategic decision – for example, to introduce the Schools Council Integrated Science Project by next September, without consideration of its implications for other subject areas and the balance of the whole curriculum. But if the first steps are based on a view of the normative direction in which change ought to go, then breadth and deliberation should characterise the process and it can call on more extensive support. It looks as if the notion of a common curriculum, initiating all pupils into a selection from the culture, is acquiring normative status at last. And this stems directly from our unsatisfactory experiences with the piecemeal developments of the sixties and early seventies.

Yet the idea of secondary education as general education is not really new. Although Morant's 1904 Regulations for Secondary Schools (quoted in Maclure, 1965) led directly to the cellular grammar-school subject-based curriculum, and so ultimately to the cafeteria curriculum of the first-generation comprehensive, this was certainly not the original intention:

The instruction must be general; i.e. must be such as gives a reasonable degree of exercise and development to the whole of the faculties, and does not confine this development to a particular channel, whether that of pure and applied Science, of literary and linguistic study, or of that kind of acquirement which is directed simply at fitting a boy or a girl to enter business . . . Specialization . . . should only begin after the general education has been carried to a point at which the habit of exercising all these faculties has been formed and a certain solid basis for life has been laid in acquaintance with the structure and laws of the physical world, in the accurate use of thought and language, and in practical ability to begin dealing with affairs.

This passage suggests that in the new grammar schools, subjects were to be the servants of the curriculum – the means by which a 'solid basis for life' was to be laid, rather than the end in itself. But success at university entrance came increasingly to dominate the grammar-school ethos: and so the single-subject honours degree course cast its shadow not only on the sixth form, but on the years that led to it. The subject-specialisation lobby ensured that instead of a broad curriculum which made use of subjects, we had a narrower curriculum which became subservient to subjects. The logical development, in due course, of this subject-based curriculum was the option scheme which aimed to offer as wide a choice as possible between separate subjects. This is not to deny the considerable value of organising concepts into subject structures, nor the existence of boundaries between those structures. But what ultimately matters, as far as general education is concerned, are the concepts themselves rather than the boundaries for their own sake.

Implications of a broader curriculum

Another consequence of the haphazard changes of the 1960s is a move away from the RDD model of curriculum innovation, towards one which sees the process as focused on the school itself. In one sense, this is only to recognise that what ultimately matters is the interface between teacher and learner. And there is little doubt that too many curriculum projects still fail to give sufficient importance to the involvement of teachers. But in a wider sense, it sees the teacher not as the prisoner of his subject competence, but rather as an active contributor to the school's own great debate on education. His autonomy transcends the walls of his classroom and brings him face to face with questions of culture, value and ideology; in short, with the moral and political questions which are implicit whenever the educational good is discussed. And by the same token, the school must ensure a broad base for its decisions. Skilbeck (1976a) has written:

> The more inclusive a curriculum is with respect to pupils' experiences and interests, and the more successful the teaching and learning, the greater the likelihood of political interest being taken in at least the major policy questions.

The degree of inclusiveness means that the difference between a 'core' and a 'common' curriculum may be more than semantic. If the curriculum is seen still in subject terms, but writ larger to ensure pupil competencies in a wider range of basic skills, then it is conceivable that it could be centrally determined and centrally evaluated. But if it is seen as a system of mediation between the individual and the culture, with or without a framework of national guidelines, it means that schools cannot be fitted out with an off-the-peg common curriculum, as they could with Nuffield Physics or Keele Integrated Studies; it means that they are themselves in the business of deep-structure curriculum planning. And so we can see that the common culture curriculum, and school-based curriculum planning, are a symbiotic pair; each needs the other if it is to flourish.

It would be nice to think that the inadequacies of the subject-based curriculum, whether bipartite or core-based, are generally understood. As Skilbeck remarks:

> Such a curriculum has had value in the past and is still valuable for specialized and limited purposes, such as training the small minority of academic specialists needed by . . . higher education. What it is not so useful for is

21

mass, general education, or the training of flexible, creative, adaptive specialists to work in rapidly changing social, industrial and commercial enterprises.

But to assume such an understanding would be unwise. It is a remarkable paradox that many of those whose chief concern is to further the interests of industry and commerce — with what is fashionably termed 'the creation of wealth', but more simply and quite properly, with making money — are the most vociferous in their support for basic subjects for basic skills. Such a view would be justifiable if knowledge were stable, if economic success depended on established techniques and existing products. But the very reverse is the case: success depends on new ways of applying new knowledge. It is arguable that for industrialists to see the function of schools in such outdated terms betrays their own failure to develop new ideas and seek new markets.

For such a purpose, a broadly-based general education will be the only one that can equip pupils with the autonomy they need to go on learning. As Jenkins and Shipman (1976) have put it:

> The clue to the relationship between schooling and work lies in the different levels of knowledge required at work. The curriculum can be concentrated on basic, specialised technical skills at one extreme, and on a broad general education at the other. The former will tend to be restricted in length as well as depth, and geared to a limited range of job opportunities. The latter is infinitely extendable and divorced from links with any particular working skill.

We could add that nothing is more likely to distort a common curriculum, and reduce its value both as a device for educating the individual and enabling him to make the most effective contribution to an advanced industrial society, than an emphasis on short-term instrumental goals.

If we look at the Green Paper in this light, there are signs of an infirmity of thought and a weakness of argument. It doesn't help that the curriculum is thought of in a narrow sense:

> The curriculum is not the school's sole means of realising

the purposes of comprehensive education. The creation of a lively and caring community, where the pupils have opportunity to exercise initiative and responsibility; the sensitive organisation of groups for learning and other activities; the establishment of an unobtrusive system of effective guidance and support for the adolescent are crucial to success.

If these latter tasks are not seen as the proper business of curriculum planning, it is difficult to see how the whole resources of the school can be yoked behind a common purpose. And there are other signs of a limited field of view:

> It is not the task of schools to prepare pupils for specific jobs but experience has long shown that studies and activities that are *practical and obviously relevant to working life* can be valuable as a means of learning, including the learning of basic skills. (My italics.)

There is certainly everything to be said for making knowledge useful to the pupil; Whitehead's view (1962) that 'Education is the acquisition of the art of the utilisation of knowledge' has everything to commend it. Rather, therefore, than teach a fourth-year pupil art and craft in separate compartments (or, worse still and much more likely, allow him to drop both subjects at the end of the third year), it makes sense to interrelate them with the concept of design as a unifying scheme; and we might, as a result, find him making a model of a caravan after considering carefully the contributions that the separate disciplines can make. But this would hardly qualify as an activity 'obviously relevant to working life'. Should he be obliged, if he happens to live in, say, Middlesborough, to make a model of a bridge, or a blast furnace? Or would it not be better for him to concentrate on the 'basic skills', to unscramble the design-based omelette, and make him learn technical drawing and how to make a half-lapped joint? But this would not only be miseducational; it would deny him exactly the kind of experience which pupils need if they are to understand the nature of technology in our society.

One has the same feeling – that the Green Paper has

got it only half-right — when one reads the fifth of its 'aims for the schools':

> To help children to appreciate how the nation earns and maintains its standard of living and properly to esteem the essential role of industry and commerce in this process.

The first part is unexceptionable, but how does one teach pupils to 'esteem' things: indeed, to esteem them 'properly'? Can an English teacher inculcate a proper esteem for the works of Shakespeare? Is this what he even tries to do? Does he not rather try to develop some understanding? If the pupil ends up with a view of the Bard as critical as that of Shaw, has he failed as a teacher? This is a singularly unhappy passage, and suggests that the Paper's authors have only a third-hand knowledge of what good schools are like. One can only take a crumb of comfort from this altogether more realistic sentence: 'If more able young people are to be persuaded to make their careers in industry and commerce the remedy lies with the companies and firms and only to a minor degree with the schools.' This, at least, puts the boot on the right foot.

What the Green Paper lacks is an underlying structure of reasoning and argument. It will not do, as Bailey (1978) points out, to advance proposals which are themselves controversial, without acknowledging the need to justify them: 'A major thesis of the document is that education must serve the needs of . . . an industrial growth economy . . . But there is also a case against growth and ever-expanding technology . . .' More objectionable still is the 'common-denominator' approach to the framing of educational policy:

> Another assumption of the document . . . is that issues about the curriculum of schools are somehow to be decided by asking all and sundry to voice their needs: the needs of parents, of employers, of the nation, etc. Apart from the obvious problem of who resolves difficulties of conflicting needs and by what criteria this is to be done . . . are there no objective and fundamental principles of curriculum content, such that some views are arguably right and others wrong?

This is the real weakness of the Green Paper, and in the

long run it is likely to be remembered less for what it says, than for the fact that it actually happened: that however ineptly, the curriculum found a place at last on the political stage.

Another kind of threat comes from those who profess support for a common curriculum, but who misunderstand this crucial relationship between school and work, and suggest that 'school should be more like work'. We have, of course, been here before; and with another swing of the pendulum, it will be time to revive 'secondary schools should be more like primary schools'. The fact is that at each end of secondary schooling a transition has to be made, and the smoother we can make it, the better. But this technical problem should not be confused with that of defining and developing the best programme for an educational institution. This does not mean diluting the strength of a common curriculum by making work experience courses a compulsory component. The evidence of a few years ago was that these can be of dubious value; and if badly done, they can amount to an inoculation against the presumed attractions of industry. It is also true that if well done, as perhaps a vacation course, they can be strikingly successful. But this is not an argument for putting industry on the curriculum. It suggests rather that industry and schools should try to extend their present arrangements for vacation courses whereever practicable.

If we pause and examine the suggestion that 'industry on the curriculum' will make pupils better prepared for it, we see it hinges on a mistaken view of what industry is like. For the assumption is that school is a place of pseudo-experiences, where children learn vicariously rather than by sinking their teeth into 'the real thing'. But what is the real thing of which industrial experiences are made? It is made, unsurprisingly, of life itself: of personal relationships, of understanding Whitehead's 'insistent present', of learning how to learn, of developing personal qualities of leadership and service to a common good. It is, in fact, about the true purpose of a thoughtfully-structured common curriculum: to bring each pupil on the inside of our cultural heritage, so that he is equipped with the independence of mind to make his own judgments, and with the ability to go on learning. And it will seek to do this as meaningfully as possible, so that the school draws wherever it can on local resources in the widest sense.

We must therefore give short shrift to those who would do a disservice both to schools and to industry by allowing muddled thinking to attenuate the power of the common curriculum. Neither is it necessary, as the Green Paper suggests, that 'Industry, the trades unions and commerce should be involved in curriculum planning processes': unless this simply means, quite rightly, that in formulating a whole-curriculum policy, a school must involve all those in its community who might reasonably be supposed to have an interest in its activities. There is no doubt that many schools have been lax in these matters; there are some without as much as a parent-teacher association. It is unfortunate that the omissions of the few force politicians up the primrose path that leads to the Taylor Committee's report, and to the more hawkish passages in the Green Paper. For it would indeed be regrettable if, for example, the presence in a school's catchment area of a large joinery works meant that the head was forced to make woodwork a compulsory curriculum subject for all pupils for five years. Is this really the intention? We must assume not: but there are lesser dangers which could have pernicious curriculum effects. We have at least been warned. It is refreshing to note that Professor Dahrendorf, interviewed in the January 1978 issue of *New Fiction*, reminds us that the young should read novels 'to understand what life is about, to provide their maps'. For we are, at bottom, concerned to see the curriculum as a map of our culture; and the day when novels go out of the window as 'work experience' comes through the door will be the day to give up hope for us all.

We can conclude by summarising the general argument. Curriculum change reflects change in society, and the mood of change for novelty's sake is over. Instead, we see a search for coherence, and this is reflected in a move towards planning the curriculum as a whole. Along with this goes a trend away from the research-development-diffusion model for curriculum development, and towards new strategies for school-based development. This implies a new concept of professionalism for the teacher, and new styles of in-service education and of interaction between theory and practice.

There are dangers that the quest for a broader curriculum will lead to a 'core' curriculum, relating to the content of teaching rather than the nature of learning. They arise from a narrow, Luddite-like view of the autonomy of the teacher, and from a misunderstanding of the style of education appropriate to an industrial society where to survive is to adapt. But if the notions of the common curriculum and of school-based curriculum planning can be exploited for their mutual richness, there is every hope that schools can generate a curriculum which, as Reynolds and Skilbeck (1976) argue,

> may be thought of as a kind of map or chart of the experiences, thought processes and life styles that we regard as worth while. What is common about it is its generality, universality and communicability; it is capable of being shared, enjoyed and valued by all.

To achieve this will require fresh thinking about the roles of teachers and heads, of linkage agencies between the school and other educational centres, and of the school itself as an agent of curriculum change. In the next chapter we shall make a start by looking at how the new direction of curriculum change might determine the school's approach to its curriculum and organisation, and how the school can become a creative centre for promoting and sustaining change.

Chapter 2

School and Curriculum

Our task is to examine the process of curriculum change in the school, and we have been led to focus our attention on the school itself. At the same time, the story of curriculum development over the last fifteen years shows plainly enough that schools are more likely to follow than to lead. And the kind of lead they are given will take account of what seems socially desirable, and of what seems practically possible. Until about 1976, what seemed best on both counts was piecemeal development, reflecting the division of pupils into ability groups and the division of the curriculum into subjects. Curriculum coherence was less important than the freedom of pupils, particularly 14–16 year olds, to choose subjects and courses; and the freedom of teachers to choose between externally developed curriculum projects. This cafeteria approach suited the arbitrary way in which comprehensive schools were being put together from the grammar and modern traditions, and also suited a subject-centred view of curriculum and teacher professionalism. No one seemed much concerned to expose the key questions of curriculum design and control: 'Professionals and laymen alike have joined in keeping the public curriculum away from any public forum or debate' (Becher and Maclure, 1978).

The whole curriculum

The new emphasis on the curriculum as a whole is doubly important for the change process. First, it means that *per se* any proposals for change must be tested against the unity of the whole curriculum, and so must widen the participation of both teachers and developers beyond the boundaries of subject and specialism. Second, it implies a process of culture selection and transmission which will not only involve teachers in new kinds of professional activities; it will also extend the basis of judgment beyond the teacher and the school to the LEA and to national agencies. It is not as if we are simply replacing an old set of aims with a new model: we are changing the kind of innovation, the process of innovation and the very basis for determining the form of the innovation. The doors of the public forum are open, and education is very much on the agenda.

It will, of course, always be true that the process of innovation will be determined by the kind of innovation we have in mind. Bolam, for example (1974), has suggested four general factors in the management of innovation: the innovation; the innovator; the innovating system; 'all of which interact with, and are changed by, each other during the time period (factor 4) of the innovation itself'. The extra factor in this case, which makes the years ahead so interesting for the secondary curriculum, is that the sought-after innovation of whole-curriculum change permeates every aspect of school life, and queries every assumption on which present practice is based. This is brought out clearly by some pointed questions posed, shortly after the publication of the Green Paper, by the Senior Chief Inspector of Schools (Browne, 1977):

> To take the whole curriculum, can it be right that the experience of pupils in our secondary schools and even in the same school is so diverse? . . . Is there really no such thing as a secondary curriculum proper for all pupils? . . . For all pupils, does [the traditional curriculum] sufficiently foster the knowledge, skills and qualities of mind and feeling that would serve — and here one takes off into the rather grandiose world of educational aims — society, the country's interests, and our own very small world?

It is one thing to acknowledge that, in the post-1976 climate, the answer to all these questions is, *tout court*, no: the certainty of this response is the best reason for asking them. But it is quite another to frame a reply in curricular terms, and suggest how we might implement it. And the interactive nature of the change process means that unless we form a reasonably clear idea of what it is we would like to see happen, then we cannot rationally expect to say how we can make it happen. We have, though, examined in Chapter 1 the pattern of events which has led to the notion of a common curriculum or, as Browne puts it, 'a secondary curriculum proper for all pupils'; and we have considered at some length the need for clearer thinking about the link between school and society than the Green Paper's assertions about the values to pupils of activities 'obviously relevant to working life'. And we have concluded that there is no gainsaying the central function of the school to mediate the culture in an effective way for all pupils. We have, as it were, cleared the decks for a closer study of what kinds of questions and strategies lie ahead: and we have seen that we must seek not detailed prescriptions and cut-and-dried solutions, but rather to explore the territory, examine the pitfalls, try to identify the right paths and the equipment needed to follow them. The influence of the past will be inescapably with us, and we must try to learn from it and not be misled by it. We have already delineated its general characteristics, but we shall need to look more closely at those aspects which have a more direct and specific bearing on curriculum change.

In this chapter, our frame of reference is the school, and our concern is with the ways in which forces for change can arise internally and might be exploited. We shall assess the influences which, in the general context of whole-curriculum change, might deflect in one direction or another, and look also at attempts to analyse and stimulate the change process in the school. In subsequent chapters we shall shift our focus to the implications for teachers and the learning process, and for heads and the external influences on the school. But for the moment, we must see how change might start with teachers themselves, and the considerations that arise when the school begins to give its curriculum greater coherence. This will involve a look at theoretical approaches and the practical context in which they must be judged.

The perceptions of teachers

Let us put practical considerations first, and set the scene by looking at two examples — taken from real events — which show how teachers can influence the curriculum. The central figure in the first example is the head of history, newly arrived in a traditionally organised comprehensive school. His concern is less with a body of content for its own sake, and more with giving pupils an insight into the nature of historical understanding by examining, for example, the concept of evidence. His enthusiasm infects the second in the department, who responds with a local history project and helps establish a history resource centre. Within a few months the head and deputy are involved; double periods are requested for first-year history in the following academic year, and tables in place of locker desks. And the history department's advocacy of non-streaming in the first year has gained the support of other staff. In particular, an *entente* has sprung up with the English department, and plans are laid for interrelating their work in the first and second years. The extension of such a scheme to geography is obvious; but the head of that department is a mature teacher, well known as a subject examiner and jealous of interference in subject matters.

On any commonsense view, the educational aims of the revitalised history department are worthwhile, and are matched by the quality of the teaching and the enhanced pupil engagement. But they make waves: ripples of discontent are spreading beyond the first year, and the head of history argues that his subject offers pupils an access to aspects of our culture which should make it not an option in the fourth and fifth years, but a part of the compulsory core along with English, religious education and physical education.

The Shane-like arrival of one teacher has catalysed forces for change which were hitherto latent. The school's creative response could take shape in subject terms. No doubt a compromise could be worked out which, perhaps, retained the existing scheme of options in the fourth and fifth years and banding in the second and third, but unstreamed the first year and gave the history and English departments

31

double periods, adjacent classrooms and better resources. But one could put a different interpretation on events. At a deeper level, questions have been raised about the grouping of pupils, and about the relationships between subjects; at root the structure of the whole curriculum in the school has been challenged. The new state of affairs could become the departure point for a fundamental review of the curriculum.

In this example, the new teacher has sought simply to create the kind of conditions in which he and his department can flourish. He has taken his past experience, mapped it onto the new pattern and examined the fit. In the next example, we see a new teacher applying the same pragmatic approach not to subject teaching, but directly to matters of curriculum design. Some eighteen months after joining a new comprehensive school as head of the sixth form, he has circulated a mimeographed paper to the head and staff that form the school's management committee, headed 'option schemes in the fourth and fifth years'. His previous post was as head of history in a school operating an 11−16 common curriculum, and his paper is an instinctive, uncommissioned response to the traditional core-plus-options scheme which he is now encountering for the first time.

The first point he makes is that the new school 'values the independence of its subject departments'. But:

> Option schemes seriously undermine this autonomy because they have a habit of throwing up strange assortments of pupils who do not fit neatly into any of the examination and syllabus schemes prepared by departments . . . since the numbers of children opting for a subject will inevitably vary from year to year, departments cannot plan ahead accurately . . . even strongly structured option schemes will produce some very small and some very large classes . . .

The writer goes on to list further disadvantages. Option schemes always result in a hierarchy or class-structure of subjects; timetabling the options is an onerous task; and pupil choice is in practice largely illusory. He then gives the advantages of a curriculum in which 75 per cent or so was taken up with a common curriculum, and concludes:

This is not the place to discuss the details. Everyone will have his own preferences although I would be very surprised if we do not come to a high degree of consensus about what subject areas we feel 14 year olds ought to learn. For the pupils there will be choice within a subject area rather than between subjects . . . perhaps, but not necessarily, a choice between syllabuses; certainly some choice between topics and a variety of learning methods and materials to suit individual requirements. At least these are goals to be aimed at, if not capable of immediate realisation.

Although the new teacher is arguing a case which in my view deserves support, what is more interesting is not the argument for its own sake but the way he has gone about it. It discusses the unsatisfactory aspects of present practice, and in doing so brings up some points which had certainly not occurred to me even though the drawbacks of option schemes have been a personal concern. There is, in short, no substitute for the perceptions of the informed teacher who sees his professionalism not in a narrow, subject-limited way but who rather uses his subject specialism as a power base from which to survey and, indeed, modify the whole curriculum. The first point, about departmental autonomy, uses the school's policy position and his own role in the school as an effective springboard for his argument. And the conclusion, by the same token, emphasises that this is merely the beginning; the new teacher realises that change is a slow process, and one which must respond to the school's own constraints and aspirations. But it stresses the wider goals and a consensus approach to a new solution.

Possibly because the writer was fortunate in having had experience of the alternative scheme he proposes, the tone of the document shows that he regards this alternative as being in the realm of the possible; it is not eccentric or far-fetched, but responsive to a shift in mood and climate which urges at least serious consideration. It thus illustrates the most likely way in which curriculum regeneration can be instigated: by the active leadership of lively teachers who sense that normative strategies can be used to bring about distinct and coherent change. Often it will be the task of heads to write papers of this kind: but any head should be delighted to find the job done for him. There could be no clearer indication that the timing is right. His responsibility will then be to establish the conditions for dialogue, debate and staff development.

How far these conditions are met and utilised will depend on the school's capacity to respond, and this is often said to be a measure of the school's creativity. Thus Nisbet (1973):

> The term 'creativity' is carefully chosen, for it is a quality of the intellect; and the quality we seek to assess is an intellectual quality of the school . . . Creativity . . . is not just a quality of unique individuals or of unconventional institutions, but a style of problem-solving . . . The creative teacher is often the divergent personality who likes to work on his own . . . the creative school must somehow release these talents (or sometimes, restrain or redirect them) so that they are shared with colleagues and made available more widely.

The difficulty with this approach is that — just as when we apply the label 'creative' to a person — it tells us little about how to become creative. White (1972) has given a useful philosophical analysis of the term:

> To say that a person is 'highly creative' is not very informative unless it is clear in what area of activity he is creative . . .'Creative' . . . picks out not something about a person's inner processes, but about what he publicly produces . . . A creative thinker is one whose thinking leads to a result which conforms to criteria of value in one domain or another.

So while there is no harm in talking of 'the creative school', we must note a certain circularity in the term. We can apply it to a particular school in virtue of the observable products of its processes of innovation, but we are still left with the task of determining those processes. And because creativity cannot exist in a vacuum for a school, any more than it can for a person, there is a danger that to pursue it for its own sake could be misleading. We need to know what it is that the school is expected to be creative about: different styles of curriculum change entail different patterns of interaction and invention.

The perceptions of researchers

I have suggested that the approach of teachers themselves to these matters is pragmatic rather than analytic. But from the point of view of researchers who stand outside the school and seek to understand why and how it can become creative, analytical methods come easily to hand. In the language of innovation management, it is a matter of looking at the school as the innovating system or user organisation. Although these terms might, for some teachers, have a distasteful ring of the factory floor or management seminar about them, there is no reason why we should not see what good they can do in throwing light on how schools work, and why some work better than others. Before, therefore, we go on to look at how the schools in our examples might follow up their internal stirrings, we can acquire a useful perspective by examining some of the analytical approaches that have been developed.

Most of this work has been done in North America, and it relies heavily on a systems approach to the school and its functioning. In general, this means that the field under examination is seen as a closed system that can be characterised by determining the elements of its input, output and of the intervening process. Determining these attributes or objectives often means recourse to behavioural concepts, usually with some simplification in order to keep the complexity of the model in reasonable bounds. In this country, a study along these lines has been made by Bolam (1974), who offers the qualification that 'the framework is primarily intended to act as a heuristic and analytic tool rather than an accurate and complete representation of the real world'. We can give an idea of his general approach by noting a few of the sub-headings from just one part of his survey. Under 'organisations' we have: Structure; Authority; Roles and relationships; Complexity; Span of control; Processes; Curriculum; Pedagogy; Evaluation of Pupils; Administration; Decision-making; Finance; Communication flow; Underlying ideology; Leadership style; Health; Climate; Open v. closed; Organic v. mechanistic; Response style; Innovativeness; Creativity; Relationship to macro-system; Perception of macro-system; and so on. To be more specific, we might instance the work of Eichholz and Rogers (1964) as a practical example; an attitude survey of resistance to new educational media on the part of elementary school teachers in America. They identified eight types of rejection responses:

i Through ignorance: 'I don't know what to do if the film breaks';

ii Through default: 'I never use a tape recorder';

iii By maintaining the *status quo*: 'The book does it that way';

iv Through social *mores*: 'Only certain classes visit the museum';

v Through interpersonal relationships: 'The head doesn't think less of a member of his staff because he doesn't use audio-visual materials';

vi Through substitution: 'I get more work done with charts than with audio-visual materials';

vii Through fulfilment: 'I'm not interested in A–V materials. I'm interested in art and music';

viii Through experience: 'They liked filmstrips at first, but got bored with them'.

Studies of this kind will often use questionnaires and sample interviews to aid the process of categorisation, which can then, in a quasi-scientific way, be used to interpret the original data. But one is always left with the feeling that the data might equally well satisfy some other schemata, and that the particular choice of categories could well raise more questions than it answers. If they are too simple, they take an impoverished view of human knowledge and behaviour; if they are too complex, they resist attempts – however elaborate – to build them into simple hierarchies.

It is worth looking in a bit more detail at a better known and more ambitious attempt to apply a systems approach to schools as organisations. Miles (1965) sought to identify the factors which promote planned change, and postulated ten dimensions of 'organisational health'. A healthy organisation not only survives its environment, but continues 'to cope adequately over the long haul' and extends its abilities for coping and survival. The dimensions are:

i *Goal focus*: in a healthy organisation its members are clear about goals and their acceptability;

ii *Communication adequacy*: adequacy of communication involves distortion-free communication vertically, horizontally and across the boundary of the system to and from the surrounding environment;

iii *Optimal power equalisation*: subordinates can influence upwards, and can see that their superiors can do the same;

iv *Resource Utilisation*: a healthy organisation works to its potential. People are neither overloaded nor idling;

v *Cohesiveness*: its members wish to stay with the organisation, to be influenced by it and to have influence upon it;

vi *Morale*: schools with qualities of trust and openness promote well-being or satisfaction;

vii *Innovativeness*: a healthy system would tend to invent new procedures, move towards new goals . . . to grow, develop and change;

viii *Autonomy*: a healthy organisation does not respond passively to demands from outside;

ix *Adaptation*: the ability to accomplish corrective change should be faster than the change cycle in the community;

x *Problem-solving adequacy*: the issue is not the presence or absence of problems, but the manner in which the . . . organisation copes with problems.

Some of the weaknesses of Miles's health concept have been mentioned by Bolam (1977):

Whatever its value as a sensitising and heuristic device, there are a number of important problems . . . For example, the use of the analogy with a biological organism is open to the kind of criticism . . . that such metaphors devalue the role of individual purposiveness and motivation . . . At a more practical level, the components of the concept are very difficult to operationalise.

The Miles dimensions are at least reasonably accessible: when the management argot is simplified and the nouns turned into verbs, one can see, for example, that 'optimal power equalisation' is more likely to occur if the innovating school shifts the emphasis away from subject boundaries and towards the learning process; a recognition that new insights can come from any teacher, however inexperienced. But many different starting points would lead us to such a conclusion.

The justification for systematising the obvious must be that the resulting concepts extend our practical understanding. However elaborate the dimensions, categories or perspectives of the new structure, it must give an operational answer to the insistent question: so what? The methods of philosophical inquiry, for example, might throw a sharper light on familiar transactions, and have at least as much value as a 'sensitising and heuristic device', than the conceptualising procedures of a behavioural science which is not only far from exact, but may often be inappropriate and inadequate for the task. Those whose business is to implement change in schools may incline to view systems approaches with a degree of circumspection.

Models of curriculum change

One is led to conclude that, in any event, the process of promoting planned change in any organisation as complex as a school is more likely to yield to patient and pragmatic inquiry than to the grand sweep of generalisation. Indeed, a review of literature and research has prompted Skilbeck (1971) to declare:

> Several thousand years of practice, a rather lesser period of theory and a half century of research have not yet yielded a single over-arching strategy for curriculum innovation which rises much above the level of platitude and common sense.

Even so, there is always room for modest attempts to summarise patterns of intervention and innovation, and a useful systems model of 'knowledge dissemination and utilization' has been devised by Havelock (1969). We have already encountered the first of his three models, in describing the chief mode of curriculum development in the 1960s: that of *research, development and diffusion*. Its underlying logic, as Becher and Maclure (1978) point out, is 'intuitively attractive' to the developer:

> It first asks what are the underlying aims of teaching that subject with whose development it is concerned. Next it considers what is known about the best methods of achieving those aims. Finally, it applies those methods to the presentation of the required subject content.

In Havelock's description, the model rests on five major assumptions:

i   A rational sequence in the evolution and application of an innovation;

ii Planning, usually on a massive scale over a long timespan;

iii Division and coordination of labour;

iv A more or less passive but rational consumer who will accept and adopt the innovation if it is offered to him in the right place at the right time and in the right form;

v   A high initial development cost, compensated for by the long term benefits of the innovation.

Eraut (1972) has suggested that 'the research stage has been much less emphasised in the British context', and Bolam (1974) that Havelock 'appears to pay insufficient attention to the problems of the user system'. Guba and Clark (1967) describe this model as a four-stage process: research-development-diffusion-adoption. But the essence of this RDD model is that the impetus comes from the initiators, and it is popular with planners and administrators. We have noted its importance as the principal strategy for most Nuffield and Schools Council projects.

Apart from the difficulty of specifying aims, it is hard to find ways of determining good teaching methods that are much better than anecdotal. And above all, the diffusion stage depends on the support of teachers who have shared nothing with the developers, and yet must re-interpret the project materials if pupils are to learn from them. Such centre-periphery approaches to innovation, in Schon's term (1971), have the technocratic defects of seeing know-ledge in pre-packed units, and dehumanising the role of the teacher.

This 'top-down' element remained evident in virtually all Nuffield and Schools Council projects, but later projects, like Nuffield Junior Science and Junior Mathematics, loosened the structure to allow more teacher involvement: two-way rather than one-way communication. The central team saw itself less as a factory for expert materials, and more as a servicing agency. Publications were more likely to be directed at teachers than pupils. Account was being taken of Havelock's *social interaction model*, which essentially attempts to describe the patterns by which innovations diffuse through a social system. Its characteristics are:

i The individual user belongs to a network of social relations which largely influences his adoption behaviour;

ii His place in the network (central, peripheral, isolated) is a good predictor of his rate of acceptance of new ideas;

iii Informal personal contact is a vital part of the influence and adoption process;

iv Group membership and reference group identifications are major predictors of individual adoption;

v The rate of diffusion through a social system follows a predictable S-curve pattern: very slow at the beginning, followed by very rapid diffusion, followed in turn by a long late-adoption period.

It is a useful model to describe the spread of new methods or new patterns of organisation, like school resource centres or multiple option schemes. Teachers' centres and professional organisations are important agencies for promoting interaction, and the attitude of the head and LEA advisers will be influential.

As a basis for development projects, this 'periphery-periphery' model shifts the locus of change from the central team not to the school, but to intermediate agencies of interaction. But communications between schools, teachers' centres and LEA advisers are patchy at the best of times. In effect, the project team remains the energising force, and when funds cease and the team breaks up, there is little left to keep things going.

With both these models, it is difficult to see how they can be used for innovation which goes beyond separate subjects to the renewal of the whole curriculum: from subject-based development to what is sometimes termed system-based development. The centre of attention must then be the individual school, since that is what we are trying to change, and its dynamics are hardly accessible to a national project team, or for that matter to an intermediate group unless it has organic links with the school. We will find it helpful to abandon both the centre-periphery and periphery-periphery models for the moment, and look instead at the *problem-solving* or periphery-centre model. Its intention is to describe a patterned sequence on the part of the user. The *need* is articulated into a *problem* diagnosis, leading to a *search* and *retrieval* of ideas to formulate the innovation. *Internal resources* are fully utilised and *self-initiated* innovation is the aim. The role of an outside agent will be *non-directive* and consultative. The assumption is that self-initiated innovation will have the strongest user commitment and the best chance of survival.

A model of system-based change

This third problem-solving model can be used for subject-based development. Aspects of it can be descried in the Schools Council General Studies Project, which produced adaptable materials developed originally from a bank of items devised by teachers. But because, in an interactive institution like a school, one problem leads to another and a subject-based inquiry can easily outgrow its bounds, it more naturally fits a development process which is system-wide, and – in the case of the school – has the whole curriculum as its arena. With hindsight, for instance, it looks as if a number of LEAs relied on a strategy of this kind in preparing schools for the raising of the leaving age (ROSLA) in 1974. This was widely recognised as a chance to look at the whole curriculum rather than merely extend existing fourth-year courses for the less able, and a series of BBC radio and television programmes and booklets for teachers cut a wide and enterprising swathe through the curriculum field. LEA advisers constituted an informal resource for schools, and a variety of in-service courses was mounted. There seems to be no research study of this interesting phase in British curriculum development, which is a matter for regret: it would have been a worthy Schools Council project in itself. But we can venture that it would have revealed little fundamental change in school curricula, and we can say why: system-based problem-solving strategies presuppose professional skills which teachers have, in general, had no opportunity to acquire.

What it comes down to is that what is seen, from one point of view, as the weakness of the problem-solving model, is seen from another as its great strength. It depends on whether you take a centralist view of curriculum as some-thing 'out there' which must be wheeled into schools, or whether you believe that it is not enough merely to say that teachers must play a key part in curriculum develop-ment – rather, that curriculum is defined in terms of school-based development and that problem-solving is as much a vernacular part of a teacher's professional activity as driving a car is for a commercial traveller. To the centralist, the problem-solving model is too open-ended, too hard to evalu-ate, too disconnected from course-based in-service training. But to those who see the school and its staff as the organic unit of cultural diagnosis and renewal, curriculum develop-ment means teachers working together to transform learning, and what Havelock has termed problem-solving is simply a part – albeit an important one – of what it means to be a teacher. While one view might argue that teachers, for ex-ample, lack the time and inclination to produce new cur-riculum materials, the other recognises that unless teachers do this in the context of whole-school planning, there can be no effective curriculum development and, ultimately, no effective curriculum.

We can see that three separate strands seem to come together at this point. There is the notion of the school's creative response: as Nisbet (1973) puts it, it is 'not just a matter of improving the receptivity of schools to planned innovation from a central authority; it is assumed that we want to improve the capacity of the school itself to deal with innovation.' Then there is the general movement, remarked already, towards bringing greater unity and coherence to the curriculum. And uniting these two ideas, we have the proposition that the school itself is the place where the curriculum is viewed as a process of mediating and transforming the culture. This is a position that combines strength and simplicity, and defines the frame factors for curriculum design, control, implementation and evaluation. We shall call it the position of *cultural synthesis* since it is not a compromise, but a way of uniting views about schools, teachers and curriculum.

The school and external constraints

This excursion into models of curriculum change has indicated the benefits and limitations of an analytic approach, and brought us back to our starting point: the process of change in the school. But the journey has brought out not only the distinction between curriculum development and the management of innovation, but also the possibilities of uniting them if we look at the whole curriculum in the context of school-based change. We can now turn to a consideration of the chief issues that will arise when the innovating school embarks on a process of this kind. For teachers, there are questions about their link with the pupil in the learning process, and the kind of authority structure that will favour innovation; but a central question will be the kind of coherent curriculum that this position suggests, and the way in which it can be arrived at. Our task is not to produce a solution, but to indicate how a solution can be obtained and what it might look like. Then we can go on to consider the contingent questions of how this process can best be promoted.

The main proposition is that the school, by virtue of the skills of its staff and its exchanges with its environment, is the agency by which the curriculum is to be determined and operated. In the U.K. this is what happens at present: the external constraints of public examinations, LEA advisers, DES inspectors and the views of parents and governors, interact with a set of shared professional assumptions about the curriculum to produce individual school curricula which differ greatly in detail, but have many similarities of structure and organisation. One would be unlikely, for example, to find a school with two daily teaching periods of three hours each, or without any physical education on the timetable — although there would be nothing unlawful in such an arrangement. Schools are similar because first-generation comprehensive schools have emerged from existing models of secondary schooling, and reflect prevailing social and cultural patterns as much as any other public service. Whether a school is in a remote Yorkshire dale or a crowded metropolis, it cannot escape the consequences of mass communications and bureaucratic procedures — to use the term in a non-pejorative sense. The fact is that an array of forces, whether or not backed by legislative sanction, is brought to bear to ensure that differences are contained within an acceptable framework.

Furthermore, these externally-generated forces of conformity are in effect a substitute for internally-generated forces of conscious planning. Why bother to pull the curriculum to pieces and start all over again, when an acceptable programme defines itself, and is as a result that much easier to defend? The education systems of advanced industrial countries are bound to be resistant to change, because inertia in the face of demands for cultural renewal is an instinctive response created by the culture itself. So, in general, differences of curricular detail between schools will reflect a kind of randomised idiosyncrasy rather than different forms of systematic planning. How acceptable such an approach will be in the long run will depend on the merits of the initial components from which the institutions have evolved. In the case of comprehensive schools, the input components of grammar and modern schools were deficient in important ways, and evolution proceeded without any coherent guidance. Political and administrative factors predominated, and any educational input was diffidently offered as the project-based updating of subjects, with schools left to choose what they fancied. Little wonder, then, that the result is a system of chaotic detail within broadly similar frameworks, but which has prompted the kind of questions posed in the earlier quotation from the Senior Chief Inspector of Schools.

We can, however, see that the same forces which inhibit planned innovation and favour haphazard change would have an important stabilising and trimming effect if schools were, as a result of new inputs, to embark on whole-curriculum planning. In the short term, perhaps, errors of judgment or sensitivity might cause the occasional hiccup; but restoring forces would ere long be brought to bear and corrective action would result. Two examples come to mind. One is of a comprehensive school with shared community facilities which attracted adverse publicity when an English teacher used unconventional methods. A subsequent official inquiry vindicated the school completely: but it is interesting to note that a contributory cause of the original unrest was the school's abolition of GCE O-level examinations in favour of CSE throughout. While this is a perfectly defensible educational step, it must be judged in the light of popular prejudice, however ill-informed that might be considered to be. The autonomy of the school is, in short, subject to unwritten limitations once the prevailing norms are called into question. Another illustration of this has been publicly chronicled in the Open University *Portrait of Countesthorpe College* (1976), where the new head of what is, remarkably enough, described as a community school notes the gap between 'the democratically structured school . . . and the expectations of parents, who are accustomed to autocratic headship'. The difficulties of reconciling participatory school decisions with the more conventional views of parents on such issues as smoking and uniform are painfully evident. A parent's letter to the principal catches a poignant note of anguish and puzzlement, when she writes: 'This is the point to pause, to tap on the bland, blank wall and discover the places where it gives a hollow ring.' And in the event, decisions were modified, and there emerged 'instant traditions and working procedures which have enabled new, less stressful, management techniques to evolve' (Becher and Maclure, 1978).

The immediate point is that fears that school-based planning will lead to extreme solutions on a wide scale take little account of stabilising forces or teacher conservatism. This is not to say that a formal national context for the whole curriculum would be unhelpful, and I shall consider the operational aspects of national and local planning in subsequent chapters. One obvious advantage of a national framework is that it would define a perspective against which maverick incidents could be viewed, and thus prevent premature judgments which would burden all new departures with the errors of the few. Since the Black Papers of the early seventies, there has been a tendency in some quarters to brand all curriculum innovation as wild, muddled and politically motivated. Mr Callaghan's great debate was plainly intended to lance this boil to some extent, and it has largely succeeded. The notion of a common curriculum has moved into the central ground, and schools can address themselves to a consideration of how to derive it.

Making a selection from the culture

If we are seeking a model of cultural synthesis, we must start with the culture and see how it can be transformed into curricular experience; the curriculum, in other words, becomes a map of the culture. A closely-argued design along these lines has been offered by Broudy, Smith and Burnett (1965) who, under the heading 'demands of the culture' make a distinction between vocation, citizenship and self-cultivation. This is discussed, along with the general problem of determining the shape of a common curriculum, by Lawton (1975). Other factors in the Broudy, Smith and Burnett model are the uses of knowledge, and psychological questions of teaching and learning. Their resulting plan for general education comprises: *symbolic skills* (language, mathematics); *basic concepts* (in science); *developmental studies* (of life, social institutions, contemporary culture); *value exemplars* (art, literature, religion, philosophy as sources); and *social problems* of a complex nature, taken from contemporary life.

Skilbeck (1976a) has suggested that the Broudy, Smith

and Burnett scheme gives undue emphasis to academic concerns, and he advances an alternative cultural map as the core of a common curriculum. It 'will be based upon and will incorporate a critical analysis of the main features and tendencies of contemporary culture', and will include:

i Typical work situations and modes of economic operation;
ii Social rules and patterns of social meaning (norms of conduct, value systems);
iii The major human symbolic systems of language, mathematics, scientific thinking, religion, the arts, etc.;
iv Leisure and recreational interests;
v Institutional structures;
vi Government and social policy;
vii Forms of interpersonal relationship;
viii Modes of individual expression and creativity.

In addition, a second or optional part 'will include much of what appears at present within the examination syllabuses'.

The difficulty for schools in working out such an approach is to separate the complex strands that make up cultural experience and use them to weave the fabric of individual curricula; as Reynolds and Skilbeck (1976) ask,

How can the traditional selection of formalised culture . . . be coordinated with children's ways of thinking? . . . Can we find common denominators in both the detached, critical use of symbols which underlie the stylised outcomes of the sciences, arts and humanities; and in the everyday thought and feeling of ordinary people?

Even though activities of this kind form no part of in-service or pre-service training at present, teachers with the necessary talent and breadth of cultural vision certainly exist. But there are unlikely to be many of them, and then there is the task of organising teams and developing the kind of infrastructure which can make a unified, effective curriculum from these individual efforts. Leadership skills of this kind have not been fostered in the formation of comprehensive schools, where management has been seen in terms of industrial techniques of mechanism and organisation rather than the selection and transmission of values in education.

An alternative way of making a selection from the culture is to see it not as a whole to be transformed and mapped, but to define it as a set of acquired experiences. This is an analytic approach, and the contributions of philosophers of education are likely to be helpful. An influential view is that of Hirst and Peters (1970), who argue that the prime educational task is to initiate pupils into forms of rational understanding, determined by an analysis of the established fields of knowledge and inquiry. By applying tests of their underlying knowledge and structure, Hirst (1975) has formulated seven distinct forms of knowledge and understanding: mathematics, the physical sciences, knowledge of persons, religion, literature and the fine arts, philosophy and moral education. Three points need to be made about Hirst's approach. First, it is not a curriculum plan as such − it is rather a way in which certain curriculum activities can be justified. Second, its justification rests on a carefully-defined view of rationality: 'rational consideration of a curriculum demands clarification of the ends prior to determination of the appropriate means, for without a grasp of ends, the significance of the ends *as* means cannot be grasped.' The notion of ends is not one of behavioural objectives, and it is misleading that the term 'rational curriculum planning' has become associated with a behaviourist approach. As Sockett (1976) observes, Hirst

> can incorporate the process model within his account of the means-end approach . . . by widening the scope of our talk of 'means-ends' and by pressing for justification of ends and of means.

Third, although the differentiation of seven distinct forms of knowledge can be dismissed as reductionist ('why not seventeen, or seventy'), and the epistemology of the operation is open to criticism, the strength of the approach lies not so much in the distinct forms as in the insight it gives the teacher into the process of justifying curriculum decisions, and the clear way in which its arguments are expressed. In any case, Hirst has acknowledged from the first (1965) that:

the dividing lines that can be drawn between different disciplines by means of the four suggested distinguishing marks are neither clear enough nor sufficient for demarcating the whole world of modern knowledge as we know it.

It is because of the light Hirst's approach throws on decision-making about the curriculum that it is of particular value to the school which is embarking on whole-curriculum planning. It is clear, for example, that while a form of knowledge like mathematics may well find its way onto the curriculum as it stands, the physical sciences may appear as integrated science rather than separate subjects. It is also likely that other groups of subjects will need to be thrown into interrelation, possibly with the emergence of a faculty structure which would seem to be a convenient form of organisation for a school pursuing a common curriculum. And there will be other curriculum components to subsume: Hirst is simply re-interpreting the humanist concept of liberal education, and inasmuch as Hirst's forms attempt to define the distinctive modes in which mind works, the school which can effectively introduce them to the pupil is giving him the autonomy to understand – and go on learning from – our work and culture. But the curriculum will also reflect the instrumental demands society makes on schools, as well as pupils' personal skills, physical education and the development of character. And in working out how key aspects of the culture can be effectively presented across the ability range, schools will need to devise ways in which a variety of learning strategies can be deployed. We are still left with the task of cultural synthesis, and of cultural map-making: Hirst's rationale helps because it offers an underlying grid not so much of specific places, but of ways of getting to them.

I have suggested elsewhere (Holt, 1978) how a common curriculum might be devised using Hirst's interpretation of liberal education as the underpinning rationale, and how other, more instrumental elements may be introduced partly through the informal procedures of the curriculum, and partly by means of a small option component in the fourth and fifth years. The main point is that choice is introduced not as an extrinsic element between subjects, but rather as an intrinsic element within the faculties which make up the extensive common core. The advantage of such a scheme is that although it represents a major innovation, it is one which does not take a leap in the dark; Hirst's forms of knowledge are certainly not the same as ordinary subjects, but teachers can see how subject structures can contribute to them, and the supporting technology − team teaching, resource-based learning, interrelated studies − is already around to help them to do it. In this way we can make subjects subordinate to curriculum aims, rather than their determinant. The effectiveness of such an approach to the common curriculum will depend, as Reynolds and Skilbeck (1976) have pointed out, on how it is done:

> Our view is this: if schools think about how they can *use* the 'disciplines' of knowledge in order to mediate culture (rather than teach the 'disciplines' as such), then 'disciplines' make an essential contribution to the curriculum without dominating its organisation.

It is arguable, for example, that Hirst's analysis takes a narrow view of creativity in the arts, and of aspects of social education; and that the rational mind may express itself through non-reflective states like passion and enjoyment, as well as through knowledge. But there is no suggestion that this, or any other analysis, should be followed as a recipe; it is rather an interpretive guide to the school's decision making. And teachers will, as part of the regeneration process, be aware of the ebb and flow of debate and discussion on these points of theory. In this way the curriculum will have a rational basis, but can take account of the school's own strengths and constraints, and the changing views of curriculum thinkers and developers.

The reader will notice a similarity between Hirst's forms of knowledge, and the 'areas of experience' which have been specified in the 1977 HMI document 'Curriculum 11−16' and quoted in chapter 1. It can be seen, too, in the areas of the curriculum which the Assessment of Performance Unit has specified for its consideration: number, language, science and also aesthetic, personal, physical, ethical and moral development. Approaches of this kind have already been dubbed 'Hirst-and-water', and it is inevitable that the work of committees will show a tendency to blur and simplify, rather than spell out an argument with precision and force. As far as curriculum change is concerned, we must view these developments with mixed feelings. It is certainly progress of a sort, if it means that we are inching our way towards a coherent view of the whole curriculum, and so establishing a force which can discreetly but firmly lead schools to appraise their activities and try to offer all pupils a good education. But because the basis of schemes of this kind is assertion and compromise rather than reflection and argument, they are of limited value in helping schools to establish the actual process of regeneration. Over-simplifying the difficulties of school-based change can only do a disservice to this aim; either it will be badly done, or attempts to do it will be abandoned through an inadequate understanding of what is involved. There are parallels with the 1960s enthusiasm for non-streamed classes. Schools failed to make sufficient preparations, chiefly because non-streaming was adopted for the wrong reasons – as a social device rather than a way of making worthwhile curriculum experiences more widely accessible. Disappointment has turned into distrust, and schools wishing to non-stream must overcome hostility from both staff and parents. The success of schools which took care to plan this innovation is swamped by the failure of those who bungled it. A major effort of education and dissemination will be needed if attempts to establish a common 11–16 curriculum are not to come unstuck for very similar reasons.

One solution is to advocate a broader set of curriculum experiences for all pupils, but to retain a subject-based pattern and so side-step the need to identify key cultural concepts and bring them together in a variety of curriculum experiences. After an analysis of aspects of the common curriculum which owes much to the work of theorists like Hirst and Lawton, the Scottish Munn Report (1977), which was mentioned in chapter 1, comes down in favour of a scheme of this sort. Instead of the five, six or seven option choices which a pupil is currently expected to make for his fourth and fifth year courses, Munn suggests only two or three 'elective' subjects, and a much larger core, made up of seven 'modes of activity': English; mathematical studies; physical education; religious and moral education; science; social studies; and creative arts. This core takes up about two thirds of the timetable, and the needs of the whole ability range are met by offering a choice of subject within the last three headings. Thus 'creative arts' might be art, or music, or drama, or dance, or 'creative craft'; or combinations of these. In essence, the Munn Committee has baulked at the idea of making choice an intrinsic component of a curriculum area — a way of ensuring that key ideas are encountered by all pupils, but treated differently in recognition of their different abilities and interests. Instead, it has settled for choice once again between subjects, but by grouping subjects under distinctive headings it hopes to ensure a wider coverage.

The attraction of this proposal is that it does not require such a significant extension to the demands made on schools as an approach based on a cultural synthesis. It is therefore, on the face of it, more likely to succeed with teachers, and the idea of subject choice is presumed to appeal to pupils. The Munn Report declares that:

> We felt from the outset some unease about the emphasis on balance in the remit, which seemed to make this the key concept for curriculum planning, whereas we saw pupil motivation as of comparable importance . . . We have attempted to give due weight to both.

There are echoes in this of the Schools Council's Working Paper on the Whole Curriculum, quoted in chapter 1. But if the common curriculum is focused not on an abstract concept of balance but rather, as argued here, on representative cultural experiences which must be mediated by the school so as to engage all pupils in appropriate ways, then the supposed conflict between balance and motivation disappears. Both the Green Paper, and the *Curriculum 11–16* document, talk of balance as an overall aim, and this is another potential cause of misunderstanding in schools.

The difficulty is bound to arise if curriculum breadth is to be derived from choices between subjects, rather than choices within subject-areas. To say, for example, that social studies should be a compulsory curriculum element is fine, as far as it goes. But if it means – as it ultimately does, in the Munn Report – that pupils are to pick one subject out of economics, history, geography, modern studies and so on, then two important objections follow. First, it suggests an arbitrariness about the proceedings, since smaller schools will offer fewer subject choices, and in any case not everyone will get their first choice. Second, it implies that whichever subject is chosen, it will suffice as social studies; and this must be regarded as a doubtful proposition, not least because a purely subject-based approach to social studies is bound to be inadequate. The following passage shows that the Munn committee was aware of this danger:

> It will therefore be a major task for those responsible for the curriculum in schools to ensure that the contributions of the different subjects are so orchestrated that, in their different ways, they lead to the achievement of the established aims of the school. The attainment of this ideal will be vitiated from the start, and the curriculum reduced to a haphazard collection of disjointed units, if subject departments, insisting on their own autonomy, simply go their separate ways.

But given the natural inclination of all subject departments to go their separate ways, this is really little more than whistling in the dark. The report goes on to urge the inclusion, in these social studies subjects, of a 'core element' dealing with 'the political, economic, industrial and environmental aspects of life in modern society', but when it comes to saying exactly what this is to mean, it can manage nothing better than the statement that 'the precise nature of this core element . . . must remain a matter for further study and discussion.' The curious process of 'orchestration' remains obscure.

These points are important not only because the Munn Report advocates this type of scheme, but because Munn-type solutions to the present difficulties found in multiple-option schemes are already becoming popular in English comprehensive schools. It is a relatively simple matter to say that, in the interests of 'a balanced curriculum', every pupil must, in the fourth and fifth years, choose one subject from a list of 'social studies', another that is 'creative', and another that is 'scientific'. The assumption is that in place of the cafeteria curriculum, we need only substitute the 'cake-mix' curriculum: providing you have the basic ingredients, more or less, then you will have a complete education. But just as sugar is not quite the same thing as treacle, so is geography not the same thing as history. If there are distinctive aspects to historical study which need to be picked out and presented to pupils, then it will not do to omit them. And, of course, these arbitrary collections of subjects lack coherence; all we have, really, is the same old additive subject-based curriculum, which can never be more than the sum of its parts. The cake, in other words, has to be baked; the curriculum has to represent a genuine synthesis of cultural elements. So we must have doubts about schemes of this kind, and recognise that the bald concept of giving 'balance' to the curriculum can be seriously misleading.

In the light of these reservations, it is interesting to note that, in a report on a conference of Directors of Education in Scotland which discussed the Munn Report, the president of the directors' association writes (*Education*, 22.5.78):

> Opinion seems to be gaining ground that the Munn Committee too readily identified particular modes of educational activity with traditional subjects and undervalued the extent to which particular subjects could encompass more than one of the eight modes they postulated.

Subsequently, the Education Institute of Scotland — the largest teachers' union north of the border — has failed to endorse the Munn proposals, on the grounds that they do not go far enough. A report in *The Times Educational Supplement* comments (8.9.78):

> What is significant about Munn is that the proposals are based on what many regard as the best practices which have evolved over the years in Scottish secondary schools. For all this, however, it is an extremely conservative document and the EIS was bound to take strong issue with it . . . Munn has been dismissed out of hand by the EIS for failing to provide a new curriculum. . .

All this suggests that however painstakingly one might

prepare the ground for an interpretation of the common curriculum in terms of extrinsic subject choice, one is likely to run into the kind of difficulties which can only be resolved by following through the logic of the operation, as I have attempted to in this chapter, and getting down to the fine grain of cultural experiences. Once this is done, a scheme such as Hirst's offers a rationale which can guide teachers in the use of existing subject structures to transform these experiences into effective classroom encounters and curriculum outcomes. But making up different kinds of shopping lists from separate subjects as the starting point can only lead to confusion and uncertainty. It is to make too rigid a separation of ends from means.

We can certainly share Lawton's belief (1977a) in our ability to examine our society 'with a view to seeing what are the essential aspects of its culture which we all share despite our enormous difference in attitudes'. We have seen that the nub of the problem is not so much determining these aspects – the Munn Report shows that part of the job can be done well, even by a committee – but working them out as a school-based procedure. Unless ends and means are kept together, there is a cleavage between product and process which can be fatal to school-based innovation.

We can conclude, too, that a school is likely to innovate, or become creative, or show organisational health, if it sees a change process as a normative imperative. Once there is a general consciousness that the *status quo* should first be questioned, and maybe replaced by more coherent proposals, then the wheels turn, committees meet, teachers talk and ideas flow. It is right to separate curriculum development from the management of innovation, but without self-energised curriculum discourse inside the school itself, there will be little innovation worth managing. And the quality of management is likely to owe more to the extent and force of the prior curriculum planning than to organisational factors grafted on for purely management reasons. Schools have so much to learn from themselves.

Chapter 3

Teacher and Pupil

We have seen that although numerous attempts have been made to determine the characteristics of a school's organisation which are favourable to self-sustained planned change, such a complex process does not yield easily to the researcher's knife. Analytical distinctions are too readily invalidated by intuition and interaction. We must take rather a view of the whole, and recognise that an innovative climate results from styles of curriculum planning which take advantage of normative pressures to consider afresh the total curriculum of the school. Changing the valves in a wireless set will not improve the reception, unless it is tuned in to the right station: and once a school focuses on the task of mapping the culture in its curriculum, then we have a framework for judging the kind of help it needs to succeed. In the next chapter, the implications for the head and the control of the curriculum will be examined: at present, we are concerned with the implications for the role of the teacher.

In a conventional subject-based curriculum, the *content* of what is taught is limited by the implied boundaries of the subject; and the subject's validation in public examinations constitutes a kind of collateral in support of the teacher's *authority* to offer it to the pupil. And along with this implied content and authority goes an accepted corpus of *teaching methods*: in English pupils read books and write, in geography they might watch films and write, in history they might discuss and then write. Although teachers could — and possibly would — ring the changes on these simplifications, the point is that they need not: pedagogy might make changes seem desirable, but the curriculum does not dictate them. It is possible, of course, that a new approach to a subject – like the School Mathematics Project – might prescribe changes in content which imply changes in method: even so, the signs are that traditional methods are not readily abandoned.

In all these three respects, teachers will need to extend their professional role in a school which has accepted the full significance of coherent curriculum planning. First, teachers will have to decide whether this or that topic is part of a unit of work. For instance, a first-year teacher of English as a separate timetable subject can turn to a variety of course books, or select material according to his own interests and consistent with syllabus requirements. But suppose he is a member, along with teachers of history and geography, of a team which has as its aim 'to enable the pupil to investigate the relation between Man and his environment, using the skills of English, history and geography': what should be the English component of the topic of 'communication', where perhaps the development of language is traced and its uses explored, and the role of the media in society is discussed? He is involved in valuative decisions of a more elaborate kind, and which not only take him outside the boundary of his subject, but also invite him to consider the shape of the public curriculum. Questions arise about his cultural background, and the extent of his participation in curriculum decisions.

Second, there is the way in which the teacher should view his relation with the pupil. As a teacher of English, he can take it for granted that his business is to pass knowledge to the pupil. But he is now part of a different enterprise: how far does the aim of bringing the pupil to see his cultural inheritance mean that the teacher should take second place to the pupil's own perceptions? This is a question not only about the dynamics of the teaching process, but about the nature of knowledge itself. Once outside the cosiness of subject boundaries, the ground seems much less secure.

Third, he can no longer assume that his repertoire of learning strategies can be plugged in unchanged to the new system. He will find himself working in concert with other teachers: the new format demands new methods. Is there now no place for classroom formality? What are the resource needs for more individual learning? Has he the skills to produce these materials?

We can group these considerations under three headings: selection of experiences; knowledge and the pupil; and learning strategies. If we are to discover more about the role of the teacher in coherent school-based curriculum planning, we shall need to consider each in some detail.

Selection of Experiences

It is evident that we are concerned to extend the vision of the teacher beyond his subject specialism, and to examine the implications of this wider participation for the school's decision-making structure. We shall look first at the teacher's view of the curriculum. It has been suggested that the traditional concept of a subject-based professionalism has a limiting effect, and there is a good deal of circumstantial evidence to confirm that many teachers see their territorial rights in terms of subject competence rather than cultural negotiation. It seems likely, too, that the subject might be viewed in quite narrow terms: for example, there is no notable enthusiasm among science teachers to co-operate in the introduction of integrated science courses in the later years of compulsory schooling, although courses like the Nuffield Combined Science Project have a reasonable foothold in the first and second years of many comprehensive schools. The problem is perhaps in part a crisis of confidence, which centres around the place of public 16-plus examinations as a way of making teachers feel secure in their chosen domain. Science is an interesting case, since the need to reduce the O-level commitment for future putative science specialists from three to two subjects has long been an obvious reform for the traditional core-plus-options curriculum. For instance, the Schools Council study *The Examination Courses of First Year Sixth Formers* remarked in 1973 that:

It is questionable whether a balanced curriculum can be provided within an eight-subject framework at O-level if more than two languages or more than two sciences are studied.

This is plainly a pointer in the direction of science as a complete course with a double O-level certification, such as the Schools Council Integrated Science Project (SCISP). But the adoption of this course for abler pupils by comprehensive schools has been painfully slow. And if our concern is a broad curriculum for all pupils, then worthwhile science is for all: as the 1978 HMI document *Curriculum 11–16*, following the Green Paper's lead, points out, science should not be 'just for those who have the potential to become scientists'. It is therefore heartening to note that the Council of Science and Technology Institutes – which represents the separate science subject institutes – has declared that 'all children should have integrated science up to the age of 16' (*The Times Educational Supplement*, 24.2.78). But the same report goes on to say that both the Institute of Physics and the Institute of Chemistry have announced that 'separate sciences must be maintained up to O-level'. Unless a clear lead is given, we are likely to see schools introducing integrated science alongside the separate O-levels: a prime source of timetable congestion which will inevitably constrain other curriculum developments.

Some recent research on the middle school curriculum based on a study of six schools in the West Midlands (Comber, Foster and Whitfield, 1977) seems to confirm suspicions that teachers incline to a fragmented view of the curriculum. They were asked to state what they perceived actually to be happening in their classrooms, so as to assess empirically the balance of the curriculum. The study concludes that:

i   They are reasonably content with the existing situation with regard to the curriculum as a whole;

ii They find it difficult to think about the curriculum in terms other than timetabled 'subjects'; categories of experience, human abilities and similar labels derived from curriculum theory are clearly not a part of their regular professional consciousness;

iii They conceive of the curriculum as broadly having three relatively distinctive parts – the 'academic' (maths, science, geography, English etc.), the 'valuational' (social, moral, religious areas) and the 'non-academic' (PE, music, art, craft, drama);

iv They perceive that responsibility for moral development in school should rest chiefly with the RE teachers and in assembly arrangements.

One might note, too, that nearly 70 per cent of the curriculum was spent on the 'academic' subjects, and within this area, 'about three times as much attention seems to be given to language as to numerical activity'. The English middle school is, assuredly, a peculiar and inchoate institution, and our prime concern is with secondary education; but there is no reason to believe that many secondary teachers would not conform to the four attributes mentioned. This is a reflection less on teachers themselves, than on the neglect of curriculum studies in both initial and in-service training. This goes for heads too, for whom the INSET provision is exiguous in the extreme. Unless heads know how to create the climate for school-based studies, subject teachers cannot easily take the initiative. We shall consider INSET implications at the end of this chapter.

Integration between subjects

Let us suppose that a school has, however, encouraged its teachers to let their thoughts range beyond the subjects of their college or PGCE course, and to discuss together the shape and structure of the whole curriculum. Inevitably they will come to see that if the whole extent of our culture is to be encompassed by the confines of the curriculum, some degree of interrelation between subjects is a convenient device for avoiding duplication and increasing curricular scope. It can also allow more flexible timetabling arrangements. But developing an interrelated or integrated area of study involves much more than convenient mechanisms; neither should it be embarked upon because of the enthusiasm of an isolated group of teachers. Linking subjects together implies value judgments about the philosophy of the curriculum, and these need to be brought to the surface and exposed in terms of some consistent rationale. Pring (1976)

discusses these matters in detail, and suggests four distinct
rationales which can legitimately be used to justify integrated curricula: 'logical interconnection between different
kinds of knowledge, the structuring of knowledge around
themes, the integration of knowledge in practical thinking,
and the integration in enquiry'. Thus, to give examples in
that order, one might first link the perceptions of historians,
economists and English specialists together in inviting pupils
to look at the cultural and industrial aspects of the nine-
teenth century; second, one could take a supra-concept like
'man and nature' as a theme for a first-year programme that
could involve specialists in English, history and geography,
and in RE and science too; third, a field like sex education
raises questions which fit within the concerns of not one
but several subjects, and could therefore be organised so as
to bring to bear contributions from various disciplines; and
finally, inquiry-based work on, say, the transfer of energy
might lead a pupil to integrate studies in all the three school
sciences. But great care is needed in mounting programmes
in any of these ways: inquiry-based methods, for instance,
are immensely valuable but can be misleading. As Warnock
(1977) remarks:

> There is a temptation to suggest to pupils that their
> kind of research is real research . . . when in fact . . . they
> can only have looked at a minute section of the relevant
> evidence . . . Sometimes the inquiry method can lead to
> a greater dogmatism than the alleged dogmatism of the
> more traditional method.

Doubts and difficulties of this kind may well arise during
the formal and informal discussions which will precede the
adoption by the school of a new curriculum. But they may
not: there are many pitfalls for the unwary, and one can
no more assume that teachers will be bound to spot them,
than teachers can assume that pupils are bound to acquire
knowledge if one surrounds them with books. The school
will need to establish a climate of constructive discussion, and will benefit from outside inputs of the kind we
shall consider in chapter 5. But we can certainly say that
the school and its staff are in the dynamic business of in-
venting and adapting, rather than the static one of fitting

and forgetting an external project, as if it were a new kind of kitchen aid.

National projects and dissemination

If teachers do make use of national projects, they must be conceived in a problem-solving and not a technocratic mode. Schon remarked in the 1970 Reith lectures that in the centre-periphery model of innovation, what looks from the centre like the periphery getting out of control looks from the periphery like creativity. At about this time, project teams had begun to realize that they could no longer aim to make their materials teacher-proof: but at least teachers might be rendered, perhaps, not quite so project-proof. A new word — dissemination — entered the developer's vocabulary, and ways were sought of involving teachers more closely. Rudduck and Kelly (1976) speak of the danger 'of the teacher feeling he is at the bottom of the educational pile', and observe:

> Problems of dissemination are not easily solved. Perhaps the outstanding difficulty is the stimulation and support for teachers in their own professional development . . . It is to be hoped, of course, that teacher participation in national projects, together with advances in initial and in-service training will alleviate the danger . . . .

But to talk of dissemination is to imply that the life-force will be brought into the school from outside; and the sensitisation of the school then becomes a dependent process. The task of initial and in-service training is defined by external projects, and is to render the school manipulable rather than a force in its own right.

In practice, of course, the distinction is not as clear cut as this. If teachers are learning, for instance, about the ideas and concepts behind a new curriculum project, they are being made aware of approaches and techniques which will widen their school-based perspective. And conversely, if school-based development means uniformly home-grown materials without benefit of outside stimulus, the result could be just as unsatisfactory as a patchwork of subject projects. But it is important to avoid a false emphasis: talk of project dissemination can underplay the fundamental need to see teachers, in the school, as the natural focus for curriculum innovation. Without doubt, schools must be nourished by fresh ideas: even the best chefs need new recipes. But first they must have their own kitchen.

This brings us to our other concern in this section: that of the extent of teachers' involvement in wider curriculum issues. We can already see that the school will need to enjoy substantial autonomy if it is to carry out the job of cultural synthesis, and Kogan (1972) has made the general point that the degree of discretion allowed to schools over the curriculum and pedagogy is 'the key variable in determining the creativity of the school as between different educational systems'. This suggests our decentralized British system offers advantages, but we have noted that the traditional subject-based curriculum leaves unasked most questions about the structure of knowledge. Does the approach we are advocating open a Pandora's box of new participatory strategies?

Innovation and participation

If we look at the patterns of interaction that are likely to promote the kinds of discussion that bring teachers together to look at the curriculum as a whole, then we shall expect to see them in groups rather than as individuals for at least part of their professional activity. There is no doubt that a prerequisite for this kind of curriculum planning will be team styles of working, so that teachers can enrich each other's thinking. We can go further, and suggest that decision-making cannot be seen as a centralized activity, but should rather be structured on the basis of function and responsibility. Some detailed suggestions are made in Holt (1978): as an example, we can consider the operation of a humanities faculty, linking English, history and geography over five years and embracing work also in social and religious education. The head and leading staff will have arrived at this structure after a process of deliberation that will involve governors, parents and community interests as well as staff

63

committees and conferences. As a formal instrument of school policy, the head will administer it on behalf of the governing body: but it cannot be said to have been imposed on the school, since all relevant interests will have been brought into its formation. A management committee of heads of faculties and pastoral heads will generally steer it through the stages of adoption and installation. The detailed structure of the five-year scheme will be worked out by the head of humanities, along with the heads of subjects and of the year teams. Then each team will devise materials and learning strategies, and individual teachers will be a part of the process not only as team members, but also in virtue of general staff curriculum committees and, in particular, some system of representation on the management committee. This is offered merely as an illustration of the general principle: there are many other ways in which a rational process of delegation might be devised.

It is important to note, though, that the skills of leading and managing are seen as an essential part of the structure. There is no suggestion that teacher participation should operate on the shipwrecked-mariner principle that every decision should be open at every level. Not only does common sense cast doubt on the wisdom of such a proposal: there is evidence that it might be unhelpful in practice. Bolam, for example (1977), considers the argument that teachers are more likely to support innovations if they have been involved in deciding on their adoption, but refers to work in OECD/CERI case studies which 'lends it no support'. Furthermore, there is no clear-cut evidence to suggest that participatory structures will in general be more innovative. We shall return to these questions later, in considering the role of the head. For the moment, we can summarise by saying that participation is no guarantee of innovation: but that once a school has been led to an innovative mode, teachers will expect — and need — to have freedom and discretion to determine learning content and objectives in a delegated structure of decision-making. An innovating school cannot afford to be shackled to a concept of doctrinaire collectivism: for the team meeting must offer opportunities for the teacher with better ideas to win over his colleagues. Don Alhambra's observation that 'When every one is somebodee, then no one's anybody!' is a dire truth in creative teamwork, where the inspiration of the individual must be free to lead the group rather than be put to the vote.

Teaching and curriculum planning

All this will take time. We must conclude this section by noting that innovating teachers need time for talking, thinking and planning together; and in many schools at present this is very difficult to manage. Writing as a head of English in a secondary school, but with previous experience in a national curriculum development project, D'Arcy (1978) sees this as a key factor in school innovation:

> I shall only feel hopeful when I can report that next year everyone will have five extra non-teaching periods set aside for working together departmentally — in-service work made possible because every department has been allowed to appoint one extra member of staff. Why should that be such a pipe-dream?

The question is worth asking. The prospect of falling school rolls offers the chance to improve staffing ratios, but unless the head and staff share a commitment to regenerating the curriculum, the extra teachers could quickly be used to shore up the present structure. There will be no shortage of other pipe-dreams: the maths department would like a fourth, 'floating' teacher to circulate between each set of three teaching groups, so as to help with slow learners; the RE and music specialists have long wanted to run their subjects as extra options in the fourth and fifth year schemes; the languages department has always argued that until the combined O-level and CSE set is split, the results will do less than justice to the pupils; and so on. And there will be pressure from some teachers, and possibly parents, to use the extra staff to reduce class sizes; if there is a top-heavy multiple options scheme in the fourth and fifth years, there are likely to be groups of 30 or more in years 1 and 2 and the *prima facie* case will be strong. It is easy for us to see that this would only bring short-term relief, and that the real answer is to use the bonus to free staff to work out ways of replacing the option system with a common curriculum; decisions of this kind will test the head's curriculum intentions and leadership skills to the utmost, and the easier route may prove irresistible.

And there are other difficulties. Even with the best intentions, it's unlikely that the extra staff will produce the extra teaching periods when all the department is free. The curriculum day will, in other words, always be longer than the teaching day. Both sides of the Burnham committee recognise this, but neither seems keen to formalise the commitment. Yet without it, no school could run satisfactorily, and certainly no school could contemplate curriculum change. Despite one's reluctance to contemplate legislation on this issue, a move which brought INSET firmly within the normative operations of teacher and school might have distinct advantages.

Another point is that the traditional curriculum has generated an extensive pastoral structure in many schools, which has resulted from inadequate curriculum planning and keeps highly-paid teachers out of the classroom. In the longer term there is the possibility of savings here. In the shorter term, it is worth looking at the timetabling of the school day. A recent survey by the author in a sample of 40 schools showed that total weekly lesson time varied from 1225 to 1600 minutes, with most offering 1400 minutes (usually as 40 periods of 35 minutes). But there is no ineluctable wisdom in these matters; if a school were to move from 1400 to 1300 minutes, the saving with a staff of 60 teachers would be the equivalent of four teachers, or 100 minutes weekly for planning meetings.

And a recent NFER study (Hilsum and Strong, 1978) of the secondary teacher's day suggests that one could balance the bargain by saving a lot of wasted time, and thus improving the quality of classroom contact time. At present secondary teachers spend an average of 315 minutes daily in the classroom: an extraordinarily high figure which suggests contact ratios of 90 per cent or so. Yet only 8 per cent of the working week (of 42½ hours, in term time) is spent on lesson planning. And most striking of all, only 21 per cent of the working day is devoted to teaching proper, despite the long time spent in the classroom. This is a measure of time dissipated in sorting out pupils, books and materials, and the unreasoning attachment of schools to a system of seven or eight short lessons daily must be mainly to blame for this. It looks as if there is scope for improving the quality of the classroom engagement, so as to give teachers more planning time: and, of course, the two factors are of mutual benefit. The Munn Report decided that:

> None the less, the overall effect of the changes we propose must be to create a need for some improvement in present staffing standards.

Yet it is arguable that even without such a benefit, better use of existing staff could make more time available for curriculum planning. And without elaborate multiple-choice option schemes, expensive, small sets disappear and there is effective enrichment for a common curriculum that is extended to all pupils.

Knowledge and the Pupil

The task we have set ourselves is to devise a curriculum which will bring pupils on the inside of our culture. We envisage a process of deliberation which will involve wider interests in the school's community, and recognise the need for an underpinning rationale which will help us to ask the right questions, rather than offer off-the-peg answers. But knowledge changes, and transmission systems can change its values. And what seems important to us, as knowledge providers, may be a matter of indifference to the pupil as its consumer. We need to look at these questions, and at the kind of issues that arise when teachers are involved in values education as well as areas of content: in 'knowledge how' as well as 'knowledge that'.

The concept of initiation

An acceptable statement of our general aim has been given by Pring (1976):

> The curriculum ... should aim at the systematic reflection upon the commonsense beliefs of the pupil and student, and, in doing this, should draw upon those areas of enquiry which have extended the commonsense thinking of mankind into definite traditions of disciplined enquiry.

Determining these 'definite traditions' is a matter for argument. Pring, for instance, has reservations about Hirst's approach:

> In being more specific about the organisation of knowledge for curriculum purposes, either he does not do justice to the complex differences between disciplined enquiries into many different kinds of problems, or, in attempting to make sense of these differences, he provides an antecedent scheme of thought into which all these different ways of enquiring, thinking, arguing have to be made to fit.

Given, though, the limited understanding we have at present of the nature of knowledge — and the need to start somewhere with the business of organising it — it is the case that Hirst's analysis commands widespread support, and represents a great advance on conventional subject-bound thinking. I have suggested that it is a defensible basis for the task of cultural selection.

There is then, though, a further difficulty. Having agreed on some 'traditions of disciplined enquiry', we must acknowledge that there will be tension between these traditions and the beliefs of the pupil. Peters (1977) has put it thus:

> The dilemma of the liberal is therefore plain enough. How can an individual be encouraged to think for himself when he is placed in a situation in which he has to learn from others and whose control and motivational structures have to cater for those who are reluctant to learn?

The short answer to this is that the teacher must contrive not only to sustain the pupil's interest in the areas of inquiry which he and the school regard as important, but also to stimulate a reflective response in the pupil which takes account of his understandings and beliefs, and thus leads him to adopt and adapt what has been set before him. The teacher cannot be a passive agent, assuming that the pupil's perceived wants and needs will guarantee his pursuit of worthwhile inquiry: but he cannot adopt the alienating view that worthwhile inquiry is independent of the pupil — the pupil is not a passive agent, either. We are seeking to give the pupil autonomy, but to do so means initiating him into those understandings which our view of the culture suggests are important. The teacher is not just presenting and explaining, but also negotiating: he must use his humanity as well as his knowledge to generate an imaginative exchange rather than an inert transaction. The concept of initiation seems general, useful and flexible enough to describe the mediating role of the teacher and his understanding of the function of the curriculum.

All this may seem an academic debate, and peripheral to the business of curriculum change: but nothing is more central to the work of the schools than the interface between teacher and pupil. It supports the whole structure of management, administration and innovation. So we must recognise both the teacher's authority to initiate pupils into our culture, and the need for sensitivity and surefootedness if the school is to motivate and educate rather than indoctrinate. As Peters has remarked, one can 'overlook the main mechanism by means of which the human race has survived, which is that of imitation and identification with others who are more experienced. It is mainly through these mechanisms that cultural transmission takes place.' In organised mass education, these are the mechanisms which we must exploit.

Objective knowledge

In all this, we have presumed the existence of public forms of knowledge, of 'definite traditions of disciplined enquiry'. But some sociologists take a phenomenological view of reality, and argue that knowledge is 'socially constructed', and does not exist in objective terms. It follows that the knowledge of the teacher is worth no more than that of the pupil, and so the teacher's negotiation with the pupil should start with the pupil's own construction of reality. The teacher is neither an authority, nor in authority; and this would be reflected in the way learning was organised, even perhaps justifying the de-schoolers' contention that learning is society-based and not school-based.

At root, the point is to do with philosophy rather than sociology: what is being questioned is the existence of objective knowledge. The perspective of the sociologists is that because knowledge is an aspect of society, and thus evolves as society evolves, then it has no absolute form: and to give it such form is to manipulate the pupil in an alien interest. But because knowledge changes, it does not follow that it is not worth knowing. Pring (1975) offers a useful critique:

> One might say that it is the job of the teacher to introduce the pupil to the present state of a discipline in which the teacher is expert, even if this is to be superseded at some later date, both because the pupil would otherwise not grasp the principles of procedure or criticism by which theoretical change takes place, and because the current theoretical account, even if superseded, would be getting nearer the truth . . . On the other hand, the attack has got teeth. It is always possible for a system of thought, a pseudo-discipline to 'take off' in a rather arbitrary way and maintain its momentum . . . But my argument is that this need not be the case . . .

The phenomenology debate has been waged with much sound and fury, and there is an important point at the bottom of it all. But once we are clear about it, we can see even more plainly the need to initiate the pupil into objective knowledge as we understand it. The debate has a direct bearing on the interaction between the need to respect, on the one hand, the pupil's ways of thinking and perceiving, and the public traditions of organised thought on the other. The teacher's role of negotiation between these two positions depends on his understanding of public knowledge and his ability to relate this to the world of the pupil. This gives him his authority in the relationship, and shows too how it derives from a unity of purpose which makes nonsense of unsound distinctions between the 'academic' and the 'pastoral'. We can see that the assault of the pheno-menologists is, *au fond*, of little consequence because it sees the interaction in terms of conflict. But if we see it as a force for creative tension, then we gain a useful and con-structive insight into both knowledge and the task of in-itiation.

Teaching and impartiality

A curriculum which offers a map of the culture will oblige teachers to consider issues which raise in an acute form the nature of his authority: issues of central concern in society, to do with sex, race, politics, faith and morality. Pupils must be led to see the different facets of these issues, and this will involve teachers in discussion and argument. They cannot be adequately handled simply by writing in exercise books and on blackboards. And there are implications for the authority structure of the school: if the views of pupils are to be sought on these matters, where does it stop? Can the teacher on the one hand condone the possibly prejudiced and certainly immature views of fourth formers, while on the other reinforce the discipline on which the school's smooth running depends?

There is no doubt that questions of this kind loomed large in a number of schools which adopted the materials and the approach of the Humanities Curriculum Project, jointly sponsored from 1967–72 by the Schools Council and the Nuffield Foundation. My interest here is not to discuss this controversial project for its own sake, but rather to bring into focus the specific and important issue of the relation between teacher and pupil in informal teaching modes, and particularly when discussion of value-laden topics is called for. The project serves this purpose well because its commitment to the procedural neutrality of the chairman is well known, and in examining it one must face directly these key questions about the teacher's authority and the nature of the critical interface between teacher and pupil.

Two separate points arise. First, there can be no doubt that many schools which, for one reason or another, adopted the project had previously done nothing to introduce pupils to questions of the kind the project set out to illuminate. One must have complete sympathy with its aims, and only marvel that key areas of the curriculum can be so neglected. And it would be unwise to assume that in this respect, a new day has generally dawned. We have noted that these are the kinds of topics which are often best tackled by using the contributions of several subject disciplines; so a school with a rigid subject structure will in a real sense find it more difficult to get started. But there is also a need for a new pedagogy; attempts to discuss, for example, abortion law reform in a single 35 minute RE period, with one teacher and 30 fifth formers, are unlikely to offer much enlightenment. For schools used to this primitive kind of organisation, any attempt to tackle intelligibly the issues which form the subject matter of the project is bound to call for more sophisticated approaches; and what is more, they are approaches which go beyond the immediate task to strike at the whole structure of the traditional subject-based curriculum. Inevitably, then, what might begin as a fresh look at a part of the upper-school curriculum ought logically to end as a reappraisal of what is taught and how it is taught, right through the school. Little wonder, therefore, that the project gave rise to the odd shock wave or two. And one must admire the boldness and resolution of the project staff.

But the second point relates not so much to what had to be done, as to the method recommended for doing it. And this leads to a fundamental question. For the project argued (Stenhouse, 1975) that:

> democratic principles are evoked to suggest that teachers may wish to ensure that they do not use their position of authority in the classroom to advance their own opinions or perspectives, and that the teaching process does not determine the outcome opinions and perspectives of the students.

We have here a concern that the teacher seeks a rational procedure for the discussion, so that various points of view are exposed; but also there is the evocation of democratic principles to justify the neutrality of the teacher. Bailey

(1975) has examined these propositions with care, and points out that the discussion is polarised if one

> sets up only one position opposed to procedural neutrality, that of the teacher who allows people to think that his . . . is the only defensible view . . . Nobody has seriously suggested or argued that teachers should use their authority to support their own views: any responsible educator would hold this to be wrong as soon as stated.

The question is: can a teacher be committed to rationality, without 'believing that this leads to the same views on neutrality and divergence as advocated by the project'? Bailey argues convincingly that the answer is yes, and suggests that the criterion for the teacher is not neutrality but impartiality. For democratic values are embodied, in the nature of things, in the concept of rationality; to argue that the teacher should not be allowed to promote certain views by demonstrating their superior reasonableness is to take an existentialist, or at least a relativist, position on values. To protect divergence of view is a useful tactic in chairing a discussion; but it cannot be a principle. As Bailey sums up:

> The contradictory position I am urging is the driving force of the rational man, that is, that he constantly strives to build principles like love or freedom into an ever more coherent framework in which one illumines the other, or is shown to be necessitated by the other. He cannot, as a rational man, see them as free-floating alternatives from which he can take his pick, like preferences for vanilla or coffee flavouring.

Bailey's analysis brings clarity to an aspect of the teacher's role which is bound to emerge more sharply as a school plans its curriculum as a whole, and offers its pupils a broad view of the culture. And it throws light on all styles of informal teaching. For example, a lively second-year discussion on mediaeval justice and punishment might profitably lead to present-day comparisons, and perhaps reference to current reports of some trial or outrage. The innovating school obliges teachers to reveal more of themselves, because that way pupils learn more. But pupils have a right to expect a consistency of values from the school and its teachers: it will not do for one teacher to treat impartially the conflicting beliefs of our political parties, while another refuses to condemn the seizure of civilian hostages by urban guerillas. Rationality means that he must expose the variety of opinions, but accept that his experience and knowledge of the world give him authority to argue that, at the end of the day, all opinions are not equal, and that some may be more reasonable than others.

Classroom action research

Before concluding this section, we must consider a research approach which looks directly at the teacher-learner interface. This 'classroom action research' attempts to do for the teacher what organisational studies attempt to do for the creativity of the school. An important influence here was the work of Barnes, Britten and Rosen (1969), which looked at the language teachers used in the classroom and examined the function of 'pseudo-questions' like (in a science lesson), 'What can you tell me about a bunsen burner, Alan?':

> The original question requires the pupil to abstract from all possible statements about the bunsen burner, that one which the teacher's unstated criterion finds acceptable. He is presumably helped to do this by memories of a former lesson . . . It is not unusual for teachers to ask children to conform to an unstated criterion; children might participate better if the criteria were explicit.

This valuable study brings out clearly the need, as the Bullock Report on English teaching later agreed, to make the use of language 'across the curriculum' a conscious part of the teacher's role. Subsequent studies have attracted a variety of supporters, with aims which sometimes seem at second remove from the curriculum task of the teacher. In reviewing classroom research in general, Walker (1977) states:

> Such studies have tended to constitute something of a disciplinary mix, often turning to emerging areas . . . for

legitimation and support. The return of interest in phenomenology in sociology and social psychology, and the development of evaluation, of socio-linguistics and the sociology of knowledge have provided particularly popular banners and meeting grounds.

It is important to remember that just as educational judgments are ultimately political — because they are about priorities in the public domain — so also is the context of educational research.

Let us take an example of how research of this kind might work. In studying an informal junior school classroom, Boydell (1977) considers the gap between what the teacher meant and what the child understood. She goes on:

> it seemed particularly appropriate to categorise teacher-pupil contacts in terms of observable effects. The Teacher Record therefore distinguished between statements and questions on the basis of whether the child replied, and allocated questions to their specific category in terms of how they were interpreted and answered.

Thus an utterance like 'What should you measure next?' might be classed as a routine feedback, a factual recall question, a closed task question or an open task question. It is concluded that research of this kind can make 'a fundamental contribution to curriculum development by helping the evaluator . . . to explain why certain objectives are unfulfilled.'

The appropriate methodology for classroom-based research thus includes interaction schedules, anthropological description, sound and video recordings, participant observation skills and so on. The researcher's need to convert his observations into categories and concepts has once again generated its own procedures and its own language. From the teacher's point of view there is perhaps a loss of access; the promise of bridging theory and practice is likely to remain unfulfilled. But there is also a loss of generality: it is all very specific to one teacher and one classroom. It may well, however, be possible for the researcher to go beyond description to explanation, and identify technical errors in the teacher's handling of an innovation: to specify weaknesses in questioning techniques for instance.

But this kind of research can be seen to threaten the teacher, and in any case the act of observation will be a distorting and possibly invalidating influence. As Boydell concedes:

> If a teacher hosts a researcher for days on end, the relationship can become strained and artificial if the investigator withholds all evaluative comment . . . If the case for feedback during certain types of exploratory work is allowed the problem then centres round the definition of the rules governing its use.

And, of course, it is a very expensive approach: to tie one teacher up with one researcher would not be so bad if the results had a wider influence, but in general this seems unlikely. And most teachers are likely to see interaction analysis as an alien element in the classroom; indeed, the clinical apparatus of this type of research smacks more of the operating theatre than of the intuitive search for points of common understanding which often characterises the work of the sensitive teacher. Another important objection is that in curriculum development, the focus is often not so much the individual teacher as a team of teachers working together.

The Ford Teaching Project, based at the University of East Anglia, has pioneered approaches of this kind, and the project team has shown sensitivity and understanding in dealing with these and similar difficulties. The general aim has been stated by Elliott and Adelman (1974):

> The central conviction . . . has been the importance of helping [teachers] to develop greater autonomy and control over their own performance in classrooms by reflecting on the consequences, both intended and un-intended, of their actions. Sound practical judgment about teaching strategies rests on an awareness of self and situation generated by self-monitoring.

A useful summary of the project's methods is given by Munro (1977). One innovation was the use of pupils to monitor their teacher's work; another sought to enhance the teacher's own perceptions of pupil reactions by, for example, arranging for a 'go-between' pupil to chair a discussion with a group of pupils selected by the teacher, who would then be given a tape recording of the discussion. Recording techniques are, in fact, a prominent feature of classroom observation. Thus Walker and Adelman (1975):

> The advantage of records like those gained by using film, videotape or audiotape is that they recreate incidents more vividly than narrative description — narrative description requires understanding, insight, even theory before recording is possible . . . Use of a recording technique allows you to delay coming to an understanding; it allows you to separate out to some extent the processes involved in assimilation and accommodation.

They are, however, aware of the limitations of all this, and add that 'the emphasis . . . should always be on interpretation — on the meanings of events — not on the recordings themselves.'

Investigations of this kind are clearly capable of stimulating a greater degree of self-awareness in the participant teachers. But the fundamental task is to change a teacher's view of his teaching, and the fact that a teacher has agreed to take part in this kind of research is itself evidence that he is prepared to make the change. And the root of the matter is that once a teacher has come to view his activities in the context of whole-curriculum change, his adoption of new teaching strategies will be seen as a reasonable consequence. The complex and time-consuming techniques of recording and playback, discussion and self-analysis may appeal to a few teachers, and may have some value in teacher training as a sensitising device; but for most teachers in most schools, their teaching will change when their ideas about the curriculum change. And in this respect, there is perhaps something too inward-looking, too self-regarding about these approaches to increasing teacher awareness. It is, of course, a tendency of the age to see research as learning more and more about less and less; in this case, to see the improvement of teaching as a matter of recording the discourse of teaching, and formulating concepts for describing what takes place. But the approach has considerable limitations: not least, that in its *bien pensant* concentration on classroom technique, it confines the teacher's vision to his own world, rather than extending it to the whole culture and the whole curriculum.

Even so, there must be a place for closer study of the teacher-pupil link. The so-called action approach has the advantage that the teacher is himself a dynamic element in the research, and thus becomes sensitised to his teaching style and its defects. And we can agree with Stenhouse(1975) that 'it is difficult to see how teaching can be improved or how curricular proposals can be evaluated without self-monitoring on the part of teachers'. But the research mode is only one way of going about it, and it has its disadvantages. Teachers can develop a greater degree of critical self-awareness if they are obliged to work less in isolation, think more widely about their role of cultural mediation, and pay more attention to the quality of the learning process. School-based whole-curriculum development requires them to do just that.

Learning Strategies

There is nothing very new about the desire to improve teaching and learning, and it has long been recognised that classroom-based teaching too easily assumes that all pupils can move together in lock step, leading to a passive response because the teacher sees them as a group rather than so many individuals. It is widely believed that by placing pupils in ability streams or sets, teachers will more readily be able to deal with the individual needs of pupils – and of abler pupils in particular. In practice, though, it often works the other way: it is convenient to suppose that the set has brought together pupils who may be reckoned to have about the same ability, and can therefore be treated in about the same way. The 1977 HMI Report *Gifted Children in Middle and Comprehensive Secondary Schools* remarked that 'streaming is a very crude form of provision for the gifted'. We can safely assume that it is equally crude at the other end of the ability range.

Resources for learning

The insularity of the class teacher and the easy assumption that streaming is the natural form of class organisation both stem from a subject-centred view of the curriculum. The teacher's preserve is his subject, and the class is his domain. The streamed class suits the teacher rather than the learner. Yet even in a subject context, there is scope for shifting the emphasis towards the learner, and usually this is done by a greater use of resources. But, as L. C. Taylor (1972) has observed:

> Frequently, what they collect are resources for *teaching*: a film-strip, say, to improve exposition, or an article from a newspaper as a variant to the textbook. If indeed they collect sufficient pieces and pictures from periodicals and books to allow the emphasis to be placed on independent learning, the nature of the resources confines their use to those age or ability levels, or those subjects, for which adult journalism provides more or less suitable material.

But quite apart from the pedagogical imperative, we now have a curriculum argument for devising a closer match between the teacher's stock in trade and the individual learner. For our aim is necessarily ambitious: to bring each pupil on the inside of our culture, and to do it so as to cover all the key areas, and yet to make it fully meaningful to him by providing intrinsic choice of content and learning strategy.

And our pupils' expectations need not be limited by the confines of one class, intended for pupils of a particular range of ability; they are limited only by their own potential and the skills of the teachers in realising it. Furthermore, it makes sense to devise a system which will give all pupils easy access to the resources and strategies which are the palpable result of the staff's painstaking planning. It follows that if the basic unit of organisation is the streamed class, these advantages will be lost; while if the whole faculty operates within a non-streamed format, so that pupil groups can form and re-form, under the eye of the teacher, in order to take the most advantage of each pupil's individual development while taking account of social and personal factors, then greater pupil engagement can lead directly to greater pupil attainment. A streamed, setted or banded organisation is only second-best; it is in part a reflection of teacher insecurity. But the only limitation to what a non-streamed format can accomplish is imposed by the individual talents of the teachers, and their collective skills of planning and preparation. Even with a divided examination system at 16-plus, it is possible for a school to sustain such a format in the humanities, expressive and creative areas of the curriculum for all the five years of compulsory schooling.

But to do this, we shall need − to adopt Taylor's distinction − a system of learning that is less teaching-based in this narrow sense, and more resource-based. Our concern is for 'an active, personal interaction with people and things'. It is an irony that while many schools have designated a space as a 'resource centre', in most of them traditional patterns of class teaching are the rule, and what is provided are resources for teaching rather than resources for learning. At the other extreme, there are schools which have constructed their curriculum around a resource centre rather than a rationale of beliefs and intentions − as if boxes of filmstrips and worksheets can in themselves guarantee effective learning and curriculum coherence. And if too much stress is placed on the concept of independent learning, there is a danger that teachers will forget that pupils learn a great deal from each other. The teacher who modishly eschews formal dialogue with his class, and spends his time topping up individual pupils with worksheets as if they were so many battery hens, is forfeiting a teaching tool of great value at any age and in any curriculum. What matters is not a doctrine of resources for their own sake, but a rationale of the curriculum which shows how resources must be used.

Local resource projects

The difficulty is that devising really good resources for learning is a laborious and demanding business. L. C. Taylor (1972) found that a team of full-time writer/editors took 21 hours to produce each hour of usable 'package' material.

Publishers, however, are increasingly aware of the needs of resource-based learning, and the materials developed by many of the Schools Council curriculum projects can often be adapted fairly easily and with good effect. But, as Taylor says, there is a snag about externally-devised items:

> We have seen that the extensive and special materials needed will require a productive effort beyond spare-time labour; but how shall we ensure that there is still room for the creative participation of teachers? And indeed that of children, for we should remember that a sense of being subjected to detailed requirements imposed from above is all too familiar to them.

It is clear that for teachers in an innovating school, developing and revising materials must be seen as part of their professional business. Some of the ways in which more time could be found for this kind of activity have been discussed. Another possibility is a local co-operative, which could perhaps be based at a teachers' centre and make use of teachers on short-term secondments to join full-time writer/editors. Quite apart from its instrumental value, such a scheme would be of great in-service benefit to teachers taking part. Taylor describes a pilot scheme of this kind in Leicestershire, and estimates that:

> If a Co-op were run on a workaday, Local Authority scale, and suitable 'packages' were made available in English, Maths, French, Combined Sciences, Social Studies, then – assuming no compensatory savings whatever – the annual cost of educating a pupil taking all five subjects would increase by 2 per cent.

At present, the great variation between the curricula of different secondary schools – even in the area served by a single teachers' centre – offers little encouragement to a local authority to fund developments of this kind. They might, though, attract support as a common 11–16 curriculum becomes increasingly a feature of the local landscape.

An initiative of this kind does, however, exist in Bristol. The Avon Resources for Learning Development Unit was set up in 1974 as an offshoot of the Nuffield Resources for

Learning Project, of which L. C. Taylor was joint director. Its director, Philip Waterhouse, was formerly head of a local comprehensive: his assistant and the five subject editors were all formerly teachers. The only other staff are two graphic designers, an administrative assistant, a secretary and a despatch clerk.

The unit's task, as originally established with joint funding from the Department of Education and Science and the Avon education authority, was simply to foster independent learning by involving teachers in the production and use of new resources. It was seen not as a curriculum development project, but a place where existing ideas and materials could be adapted to fit in with a particular style of working. It was defined essentially in terms of the familiar research, development and diffusion model, and it is significant that in this first phase, the materials turned out by the unit aroused little interest in the schools. Even though teachers had helped to produce them, the unit was not yet close enough to the process of using them and making them work.

A new phase began when the unit turned one of the old classrooms, in the disused school where it was housed, into an experimental classroom. Using a first-year mixed-ability class from a neighbouring school for weekly social studies lessons, it was possible not only to test the new materials, but also to work out and systematise new learning strategies. The unit's staff were then able to give sample lessons in interested schools, and help their teachers develop and adapt their methods.

The unit is now in a third phase of development, and is able to continue to operate with funding from Avon even though DES support has been withdrawn. It became clear that there was little point in offering resources for learning without the systems of management and control that go with them. The unit therefore provides materials complete as a management pack, and a handbook (Waterhouse, 1978) which defines the purposes of a system of classroom management as:

> To decide what equipment and documentation are needed in the classroom for effective management; to show how these should be structurally related to each other;

to determine the location and transmission of information and instruction; to exercise control by the teacher's objectives.

In essence, the work of the Avon unit has taken it beyond questions of teaching styles into matters of content selection and curriculum planning. There are important implications here, which will be discussed in chapter 6. The key point for the moment is that by moving from a static conception of resources as an adjunct to the learning process, to a dynamic one which makes them part of school-based curriculum change, the unit has seen its approaches adopted by over forty departments in Avon schools, and an increasing flow of worksheets, cassettes, transparencies and accompanying management plans making their way to other areas too. The appeal of the management-pack approach is that it is teacher-activated, rather than teacher-proof.

The time-saving advantages of a longer basic timetable unit than the 35-minute period have already been mentioned. But our need to facilitate a variety of learning strategies makes it essential. It makes sense to arrange for four or five periods a day, with each period of 50 to 70 minutes in length. In some curriculum areas, teachers will ask for double periods, so that a whole morning or afternoon can be spent on, say, an interrelated humanities programme which links specialists in English, history, geography, RE and so on. It might be that an hour is spent watching a film, or hearing one of the team give a carefully-planned and well-resourced lecture: then pupils might go into their form or pastoral units of 25 to 30 before continuing their studies in a variety of ways, depending on their previous activities, or on the way the staff have arranged follow-up pursuits, or on their varying abilities and interests. Thus some might construct a model of a mediaeval manor-house, out of cardboard or perhaps clay; others might find themselves in a discussion group; and others might get a learning pack from the resource centre and look at copies of original documents. There is no scope for this kind of enterprise in a timetable of 35-minute periods.

Doubling the length of periods does not in itself, of course, guarantee curriculum change. There are, indeed, examples of comprehensive schools which have done this but coupled it with a ten-day timetable. This certainly means less time wasted between lessons, but really all that has happened is the stretching of the traditional curriculum across two weeks instead of one. There might not even be any change in teaching techniques, let alone curriculum planning.

But longer periods are one important device which will accompany innovation. Perhaps the key element in devising new learning strategies, though, is not producing resources or adapting project materials — important as these are — but bringing teachers and their subject contributions together in fresh thinking about knowledge and the curriculum. A head teacher has put his finger on the essential difficulty (Baxter, 1972):

> The principle of English education that the teacher is left to be captain of his own quarter-deck and make what he can of it, dies hard: this has produced an isolation of teachers from the support and reinforcement of their colleagues. It has also produced rigidity and resistance to criticism or change.

In the last analysis, we can make too much of immaculately-turned materials: a creative, committed team of teachers will improvise and adapt and generate a better teaching milieu than any number of individual teachers pursuing separate paths, however lovely their worksheets and study guides may be. And much can be done without elaborate materials: small groups can act out French playlets, tape-record their own plays based on the Greek myths, discuss the role of the professional woman, invent series of numbers and use pocket calculators to see whether they converge — all these opportunities can be realised once the inventive capacity of a team of teachers is released within the context of a well-planned common culture curriculum.

Implications for In-Service Training

Under all three headings we have pictured teachers in activities that are unlikely to be very prominent in the traditional school. They are making curriculum decisions outside their immediate subject competence, reassessing their relations with pupils, working alongside teachers from other disciplines, and devising ways of bringing new concepts to life in the classroom.

And yet we should not assume that teachers are not capable of these activities. Like all of us, they respond to the normative demands that are made on them, and in most schools mechanical routine confines them to well-worn grooves of pedagogy, administrative procedure and curriculum content. The key factors for change are to do less with technique, more with context. Given stimulating leadership and an intellectual challenge, we can afford to be optimistic about the response of many teachers.

It follows that a prime emphasis of INSET should be the school itself. There is unquestionably a place for external projects and courses: but we must acknowledge the central importance of school-based initiatives.

There are precedents for both approaches. We have noted the tendency to stress dissemination as an aspect of national curriculum projects, and Rudduck (1976) gives an interesting account of this aspect of the Humanities Curriculum Project, which involved the provision of training courses for teachers. I shall return to the role of course-based work of this kind in chapter 5. For an official recognition of school-based INSET we must turn to the James Report of 1972, and its recommendation that every school should have a 'professional tutor' whose chief task would be responsibility for the induction of probationer teachers. But also,

> Among the responsibilities of a professional tutor would be that of compiling and maintaining a training programme for the staff of the school, which would take account both of the curricular needs of the school and of the professional needs of the teachers.

This sounds more like a way of justifying the James invention of a professional tutor than a root-and-branch analysis of the needs of school-based curriculum development. There appear to have been few developments of this kind. Bolam (1977) describes a link between a teachers' centre and an ILEA school to promote an integrated studies programme, and adds:

> It was originally intended that an external consultant
> with appropriate experience, who could offer an ob-
> jective view of the work, might be involved in six or
> seven occasions throughout but, in the event, the school
> group rejected this idea.

This tends to confirm the view that the curriculum context
of the James Report is altogether too narrow to serve as
an adequate springboard for school-based INSET: it has, in
effect, been overtaken by the emphasis on a common curriculum evident in recent DES papers. It smacks of a piecemeal approach, and seems to put staff development in
front of curriculum development. 'Compiling a training
programme' suggests little more than demonstrations of
audio-visual aids and discussions on the Warnock Report.

We are really back with the old problem of seeing the
school whole. It is certainly necessary to use INSET as a
way of improving the quality of teachers, and the Secretary
of State has often stated that this, following the Green
Paper, is her first priority. But it is only half the story:
and it is not separable from the other half. The best ship-
wrights in the land might construct an unseaworthy vessel
if they are given no co-ordinated plan, and left to their
own devices. Good teachers, in an advanced industrial society, are not enough: effective education in secondary
schools also demands good curriculum planning. And the
two are linked together. As a political initiative this is an
altogether subtler task, but it is one that needs doing.

If we make the school our focus, we can distinguish
between the need for support services to the teacher in the
school, and the provision of links between the school and
external agencies. And both must be viewed in the context
of the whole curriculum. The latter provision is an appropriate matter for chapters 5 and 6. But our investigation
so far throws some light on the kinds of support teachers
themselves will require. In essence, it is a matter of time,
money and sympathy. Staff will need the benefit of more
flexible policies for staffing and in-service release, so that
it is easier for teachers to find out more about developments
in their field, easier to get together for conferences, easier

to devise co-operative efforts for planning and developing the curriculum. Time to do these things calls for simpler, more localised procedures for covering absence, and for ensuring that teachers who give up their own time to co-ordinated planning are not out of pocket. Provision for weekend residential conferences ought, for instance, to be a matter of routine.

A sympathetic understanding of the demands curriculum innovation makes on teachers would lead, too, to the provision of a grant to each school for a staff library of curriculum literature, backed up by more extensive loan services than teachers' centres can usually offer. It seems extraordinary that the idea of education as a recurrent provision for teachers has scarcely taken root: and although this is largely a matter of external linkage agencies, it has an important school-based aspect because most of us learn by doing, and so easy access to the right sources is needed on the spot.

It is clear that a far-reaching approach is called for, and that it must derive from whole-curriculum development in the school. Good leadership may get a new initiative going, but sustaining it means a supportive infrastructure for schools and teachers. The creative school is truly a learning school.

Chapter 4

Authority and Accountability

Schools succeed as educative institutions because of the people in them. We have noted the failure of externally-conceived projects which see schools as passive acceptors of new methods or updated content, and the inadequacies of research studies which see them as functional systems rather than an organic whole. Curriculum change is not about new schemes: it is about new attitudes. And it is not easy, as Hoyle (1973) has remarked:

> The most fundamental form of innovation is the transformation of the values of teachers. All other forms of innovation — in materials, methods, pupil grouping and so forth — are often dependent for their success upon a shift in the values of teachers.

What changes people's attitudes is not projects, memos, papers and circulars, but their relations with other people. Clegg (1975) quotes some remarks of Derek Morrell, who was joint head of the Curriculum Study Group and later associated with the Schools Council:

> When I was at the Schools Council, I should have found it difficult to perceive, as I now do, that the curriculum — if it exists at all — is a structure erected on a base of reciprocal personal relationships. I should have found it difficult to assert, as again I do, that in the curriculum we are concerned with human beings whose failings and aspirations are far more real and immediately important to them than the cognitive development which is the educator's stock-in-trade.

It is, of course, true in all organisations that whatever their tasks, it is bound to help if they feel involved and fulfilled. This will be particularly true if the organisation is one, like an advertising agency or a school, where its true resource is simply people, involved in high-level tasks which require imagination and commitment. (It is significant that advertising agencies are prone to palace revolutions, often when the zeal and corporate philosophy of the founders are weakened and morale falters.)

Our discussion so far suggests that the school engaged in developing its whole curriculum will have this characteristic to a further degree, because its staff will work together in a consistent framework of cultural, social and moral values. This is a 'uniform house style' with a vengeance: but it is needed to give the curriculum unity and strength. At the same time, the process implies continuous appraisal. For there is a sense in which educational aspirations can never be fully met, and once teachers take their goals from education rather than schooling, they adopt a role which accepts evaluation and improvement as the inevitable concomitant of our evolving culture.

Headship and leadership

I have indicated in the last chapter some ways in which activities of this kind suggest a move away from centralised styles of management. Traditionally, an important function of the leader has been to insulate his people from the ill-effects of change and disruption. It is hardly surprising that when leadership is directly concerned to promote change, its traditional style will alter. In schools, the main focus of attention in discussing patterns of leadership and authority has been the head, and there is a parallel here with the key influence of the top management in creative enterprises in business concerns. There is not only the historically powerful role of the head, which in England derives from the influence of Victorian public schools on the development of state education: it is also the case that if the school is seeking in educational terms some coherent, unified design, then one person's clearly articulated vision may be more inspiring than a set of general principles left open to interpretation.

At any rate, it is widely believed that 'the key role of the head teacher in the school is central to innovation' (Hoyle, 1975), and the HMI study *Ten Good Schools* (1977) endorses this:

> What .[the schools visited] all have in common is effective leadership and a 'climate' that is conducive to growth. . . . Emphasis is laid on consultation, team work and participation but, without exception, the most important single factor in the success of these schools is the quality of leadership of the head. . . . Though ready to take final responsibility they have made power-sharing the keynote of their organisation and administration.

Not long ago, this emphasis on 'leadership' would have been unfashionable. The concept is not, for example, in evidence in the Open University's *Portrait of Countesthorpe College* (1976), which brings out the influence, on the proposals of the first principal, of the student riots of 1968. One is reminded that in the late 1960s, the key words were participation, group and consensus rather than loyalty, team spirit and responsibility. By 1974 the mood had begun to change, as this quotation from an article in *The Times* (2.12.74) by W. F. Younger, a management consultant, shows:

> Studies and surveys carried out in my consultancy work indicate that most people prefer to work in an organisation where there is a sense of purpose, where decisions are made promptly, and communicated clearly, where departments act cooperatively, where individuals are made to feel significant and encouraged to develop, and where the company is considered to have panache and style. In other words, people are hungry for good leadership, not resentful of it; they will identify with managers having leadership characteristics.

It is a reasonable inference that the head of an innovating school will have a leadership style which seeks to move decision-making outwards from the centre, but at the same time reinforces the unifying concepts on which the curriculum programme hinges. The change process can easily provoke feelings of insecurity, and an important function of the leader is to reassure, clarify and convince. Jenkins and Shipman (1976) refer to work by Gross, Giacquinta and Bernstein (1971) which seems to bear this out:

> [They] carried out an intensive study of an innovating American elementary school in an inner city area with high mobility, and have suggested that the prime reason for failure to implement was uncertainty among the teachers about the innovation itself. They had no clear idea of the role they were supposed to be adopting, despite apparently careful attempts to get this across and a degree of support for these teachers that must be very rare in practice. The result was that the attempt to get teachers to adopt a catalytic role was given up.

It is not enough to set up the right conditions, explain intentions and find funds: unless ways are found to give teachers a continuing source of explication and encouragement, uncertainty will lead to diffidence and the innovative thrust will be lost. And given the important part human beings will play in the business, it is not surprising that the head of a school plays a leading part in creating these conditions.

But what kind of authority structure does this imply? The topic is of interest to behavioural scientists, and Nevermann (1974), for instance, has identified four types of structure:

i The authoritarian/bureaucratic type, in which the principal takes decisions autocratically in' a hierarchic organisation;

ii The consultative type, in which the principal retains final authority, though he delegates more and uses consultative procedures;

iii The collegial type, in which authority rests with the professional staff, the principal acts as an executive and pupils/parents may be consulted;

iv The full participatory type, in which authority rests with professional staff, students and perhaps parents and non-professional staff too.

Bolam (1977) suggests this study reflects 'a welcome increase in precision of thinking about the global concept "participation"', and this is true up to a point. But, as with all these categorising exercises, the pure types are rarely found in practice; and finding a label for more or less self-consistent attributes tells us nothing about how and why they work. We can remark, though, that the head of a school engaged in cultural synthesis will perhaps display aspects of all four styles, with consultative/collegial styles predominating. On some matters, for example, those to do with staff promotion and the school's public role in the community, he will take unilateral decisions with the support of the governors: but in the deliberative process which underpins the school's adoption of a whole-curriculum policy, some decisions will be a matter for a 'full participatory' approach. And the extent to which he is consultative or collegial will largely reflect his persona and prejudices.

Headship and management

We are likely to learn more about heads and leadership by a pragmatic study of palpable effects than by the kind of classification that can easily lead to obfuscation. A wary eye needs to be kept on much that transpires in the general field of management studies. Writing of management aspects of the head's role, for example, Snape (1972) says:

> Management tasks fall under the headings of goal identification, measurement of achievement, staff selection, development and training, forward planning and innovation, and effective organisation. . . . Modern techniques of management insist that time for consultation and joint planning be made available . . . the rewards would be seen in clear and explicit objectives, effective and systematic evaluation . . . coordinated staff development.

The difficulty is that in education it is far from easy, even if desirable, to objectify and operationalise our goals in this way, and as we shall shortly see, attempts to evaluate school performance by measurements against specifiable goals have proved either expensive, or misleading, or both.

We can perhaps summarise this discussion so far by drawing attention to what might be called the technocratic and the democratic fallacies. The technocratic fallacy is very much a phenomenon of the 1960s: Harold Wilson's espousal of the 'white heat of technology' springs to mind. Oddly enough, it often appeals to those whose background has given them no experience of technology and the natural sciences. We have noted that it fuelled the enthusiasm for national projects based on mainly the research, development and diffusion model, and it can be seen too in the methods of management science of that era. Perhaps its most full-blooded penetration into a school was at Sidney Stringer Community School in Coventry, which, like Countesthorpe College in Leicestershire, is the subject of an Open University study (1976). The emphasis on management approaches is unmistakable:

> House Heads and Community Project Managers get the programmes and resources needed for their people from the Faculty Heads and Admin Service within the overall objectives established by the Executive Team.

There are also a number of diagrams with blocks and arrows: an aspect of systems engineering which has proved irresistible to many educational writers and researchers, but which rarely illuminates their contributions. Where the Sidney Stringer approach scores, though, is in the clarity with which the purpose of the institution, and the way it is proposed to achieve its intentions, are spelt out. The need for power-sharing is plainly recognised, and it looks as if teachers are given firm personal co-ordinates of where they stand, and what is expected of them. But there is, of course, no need to adopt the language and philosophy of industrial management in order to do this: it is arguable, on the strength at any rate of the Open University case study, that the school has succeeded in spite of the management approach, rather than especially because of it.

Headship and participation

It is at least possible that the democratic fallacy gained popularity at the end of the 1960s as a reaction against the technocrats' enthusiasm for regarding people as functional elements in systems rather than human beings with feelings and failings. In its consuming desire to ensure that everyone has a piece of the action, it assumes that one man should have one vote on every matter of the least consequence, and that the participant voters should extend beyond the teaching staff to those with peripheral tasks as well as to pupils and parents. It is an eccentric view of democracy, but we can see that if the glib assumption is made that universal decisional suffrage increases commitment and involvement, then it will appeal to those with an interest in innovation.

But this is to overlook, in schools at least, the creative nature of the tasks teachers face and the need to generate organic unity of purpose. The supreme irony is that by dispersing the power to decide on such a wide scale, the individual contribution counts for less and the teacher can be left feeling just as neglected as under an authoritarian system. There are two further aspects of 'full participation' which make it a dubious prospect in schools. First, its peculiar view of democracy is attractive to left-wing extremists, who are not notably tolerant as a rule of those holding different opinions, and can be a source of time-consuming friction which might even prove disruptive. The point has been roundly put by W. Taylor (1977), writing in the context of higher education:

> A passion for democratisation and the erosion of trust in the motives and decision-making capabilities of senior staff sometimes result in unproductive wrangling that takes up many hours that would be better spent in teaching, private study and research.

What compounds these difficulties is the second point: that many teachers are curiously reluctant to proffer their own opinions in meetings with other teachers. I know of no research evidence to support this contention, but it is an observation I have heard made by project leaders and teachers' centre wardens, and it has been my own experience. The result is that a few teachers dominate the participatory discussions and unless there is vigilance, extreme solutions become policy.

There is always, too, the danger posed by apathy, the ever-present danger to democracy. There is little point in inviting all pupils in the school, for instance, to take part in the 'moot', if most of them stay away. A system of representative democracy on a class or form basis will be both fairer and more effective. Bolam (1977) refers to work by several researchers which suggests that participation structures 'usually result in more, not less, power for the already powerful management, administrators and experts'.

Participation and innovation

The only thorough-going attempt to adopt a full participatory type of authority structure in a school appears to be that documented in the Open University study of Countesthorpe College, and other writings. It is of some relevance here, because although the participatory style of management perhaps attracted most publicity, and remains the distinctive feature of certainly the school's first phase under its original principal, I. McMullen, it was also the intention to implement a curriculum based on a faculty structure and resource-based learning. And while this curriculum was derived from a behaviourally-inspired statement of objectives rather than a cultural synthesis or an analysis of forms of understanding, it amounted in effect to a self-consistent whole-curriculum programme, based on a perceptive view of the kind of world the pupil will encounter in his adult life (McMullen, 1968):

> In the face of shorter working hours and less exacting or stimulating work, he will have to develop a full life outside his working hours, one that allows him intellectual, emotional and physical actions that bring satisfaction.

And although Bernbaum (1973) quotes McMullen as saying he is anxious to achieve a 'position where the policy of the school is decided by the staff as a whole', Bernbaum also

95

confirms that 'the curriculum has been planned to a large extent by McMullen'. This probably accounts for the unity of the design as it was originally implemented.

There seems no particular logical connection between this curriculum design and the school's abandonment of a hierarchy of decision-making. One can introduce team teaching, integrated work and individualised learning – and an emphasis on personal relations – without any implied commitment to a Noah's Ark style of democracy. There are, on the contrary, strong arguments – as I have indicated – for giving particular prominence to coherent structures for leadership and authority in whole-curriculum innovation. It seems as if, in rebounding from the conventional exam-oriented goals of his first headship described by Bernbaum, McMullen embraced a self-abnegating view of executive action which obscured the curriculum design, possibly crippled its implementation, and certainly led to decisions which antagonised parents and brought adverse publicity.

It is significant that after McMullen's early resignation, both the participatory structure and the curriculum were modified, with the common-core elements of the original curriculum giving way to a greater element of pupil choice between explicit subjects. It is possible that the original implementation set too great store by resource-based learning for its own sake (McMullen, with L. C. Taylor, had co-directed the Nuffield Resources for Learning Project): although the school had the benefit for some years of a particularly favourable staffing ratio (as also, incidentally, did the Sidney Stringer School already discussed). It seems fair to conclude that even with talented staff and good resources, a whole-curriculum programme will be hindered rather than helped by full-participation styles of management.

But the key point for emphasis is that full participation has as little to do with a reconstructionist common curriculum as has full authoritarianism. The publicity surrounding the Countesthorpe experiment has rightly cast doubts on full participation, but it would be a terrible error to tar the common curriculum with the same brush. It is essential, now that normative factors are leading to a belated recognition of the need for a secondary curriculum which brings key aspects of the culture to all its pupils, that we do not repeat past errors and confuse the issue in ways which could be at least tiresome, and at worst disastrous.

Participation and the governance of schools

A more recent example of the democratic fallacy can be seen in the report of the Taylor Committee on the government of schools (1977), with its central recommendation that the governing body's composition should reflect four equal interests: the LEA, the teachers, the parents, and the local community. Again, the desire to bring everyone on stage as a chorus line has got rid not only of the prima donnas, but of any decent leading parts as well. The result is that there is power without responsibility, and not least for the LEA which must provide and run the school under the 1944 Act, but whose representatives would be unable to exert control. Another choice irony is that of all the four Taylor components, they are the only ones who represent a democratically-elected body. Furthermore, the explicit responsibility given to the governors under Taylor extends to the detail of curriculum and organisation. Writing the timetable, checking library expenditure, inspecting worksheets — it is all grist to the Taylor mill, and the head is to be kept busy submitting estimates and writing reports, for twice as many meetings as at present.

The report takes a naïve view of participation, and an unsophisticated view of how government committees might hope to influence opinion. It dilutes and devalues professional skills, and in failing to anticipate the response of teachers' organisations to such ill-conceived proposals, it makes it too easy to fudge the real issue. This is the need for the head and staff of a school to form a broad base for curriculum decisions both by giving parents and community more information about the way the school works, and by extending the scope of deliberations so as to give them a chance to offer their views and to take them into account. My own experience suggests that what most parents would like is not to interfere in professional matters, but to feel

97

that the school is interested in their opinions, and tries to keep them informed. Certainly, the Taylor report is an over-reaction: but that there is something to react to is illustrated by Circular 15/77 from the Department of Education and Science, which lists 20 items of basic information about the school which it suggests should be provided for parents. The failure of many schools even to tell parents, evidently, the examinations offered and the homework policy, has brought us to the point where the Secretary of State must spell these matters out. Both schools and LEAs have allowed the seeds of neglect to be sown, and the harvest will include such rare blooms as the Taylor recommendations and the Kent scheme for education vouchers. It is worth adding that the minority proposals submitted by a dissident member of the Taylor Committee (Mr P. Fulton) recognise the need for 'a greater degree of central planning and management within the local authority (or nationally) rather than devolution to thousands of non-elected, non-accountable bodies', and strike an altogether more realistic note.

Authority and change

For heads, what it comes down to is the shaping of styles of leadership which are equal to the scale and complexity of the school, but show sensitivity towards the variety of interests affected by school decisions and encourage the devolution of authority to those who, at various levels in the school, can be expected to exercise it competently. We could do with knowing more about the kinds of decisions and problems that confront heads, and we must consider whether there are ways in which heads can be helped to do these things better.

An approach to the first of these tasks has been made by Richardson (1975), who studied — as observer and consultant — the conversion of Nailsea School, near Bristol, from grammar to comprehensive. She saw, as the central concern of the project,

the unending struggle to distinguish between conscious

intentions and unconscious motivations, between the facts about developing situations and the myths . . . that might be woven around those facts. . . . We are here concerned with very fundamental problems about control of boundaries.

The study therefore had a psychological flavour, and drew on the systems concept of boundary advocated by the Tavistock Institute of Human Relations:

> It is my belief that teachers who are themselves prepared to examine the way in which the emotional life of their own staff groups can strengthen or weaken their capacity to work together may find themselves able to engage their pupils more fully as persons in the learning situations they are trying to create.

This approach is certainly capable of offering a coherent explanation of what is observed, but its wider utility depends partly on acceptance of a distinctive structure of language and classification, and partly on the extent to which it can be generalised. The fruitfulness of case studies rests ultimately on how far they can use the particular to illuminate universal truths. The Nailsea study relies heavily on a documentary approach: one is reminded of a review by Joan Bakewell in *The Times* (20.2.78) of a television drama-documentary:

> Man learns to understand 'how it feels' not from literal reporting such as this, but through the exercise of the creative imagination on available data. . . . I have never felt more like a fly on the wall. But flies on the wall do not think, judge, suffer or care.

The Richardson study is not 'literal reporting' in this sense, but given the chosen method and the psychological angle of attack, its insights would perhaps be more vivid if it were transformable into a work of fiction.

There is undoubtedly scope for more case-study work in innovating schools, which could well be tackled pragmatically and published so as to preserve anonymity. A particularly useful approach might be that of the non-directive consultant with personal experience of senior

management work in schools, and this might prove a profitable venture for support by the Schools Council. The point
is that the Nailsea study is one of many possible ways of
finding out more about what happens. It certainly throws
light on the tasks of management, but it is not Aladdin's
lamp, any more than any single line of attack is ever likely
to be. But some approaches could be more worthwhile, and
offer more portable conclusions, than others. There should
be room for studies by practitioners, as well as academics,
on school practice: there is a need not only for more applied
research, but for a more catholic approach to it.

The education and training of heads

The first thing to say about facilities for the pre-service
and in-service training of heads is that they scarcely exist.
Sometimes it can happen that where an educational need
has to be met in the absence of a co-ordinated plan, the
free-for-all atmosphere generates a rich variety of schemes
and courses which fills the bill: in some ways, this is true
of the growth of further education provision during the
1960s, which was pretty arbitrarily demand-based but
added up to a really extensive service. But the same cannot
be said for any aspect of the training of teachers or head
teachers. And it is important to bear in mind that the heads
of innovating schools will need to acquire all the additional
competences we have ascribed to teachers, as well as the
further skills of leadership.

We must recognise that there will be as important a school-
based element in this for heads as for teachers, and this
aspect is best left to the next two chapters. But it is timely
here to look at the matters which should perhaps be dealt
with under the heading of INSET for head teachers. We
can begin by distinguishing between what might be termed
the 'in-tray' aspects of management, and higher level decision-
making which looks beyond day-to-day routine to fundamental questions about education and curriculum. My
impression is that in general, LEA and other short courses
on management for heads – which tend to be spasmodic
affairs, often dependent on the head's own initiative – have

made some attempt to tackle the former, but have scarcely touched on the latter. This is not surprising, since the emphasis during comprehensive reorganisation has been on what, how and where, rather than on why. It is really only when the curriculum is seen as an entity shot through with political and cultural assumptions, rather than a collection of subjects that have more or less always been around, that one perceives any need to train heads to do more than avoid putting their foot in it when Celia's mother complains that the sex-education textbook is immoral and disgusting.

An enterprising development has been the establishment of education management courses in some polytechnics, but these will tend to regard education and curriculum questions as peripheral rather than central, and to emphasise industrial management techniques which are relevant, if at all, to the routine part of the head's work. Other local initiatives have been taken by university institutes of education, sometimes with the offer of school-based courses as part of the programme in further professional studies. But it is all haphazard and unplanned, and there seems to be no recognition at the national level that if heads are as influential in regenerating the curriculum as our investigation suggests, and the HMI study confirms, then something ought to be done to make them as effective as possible.

A number of suggestions have been made. One is that heads should be appointed on renewable fixed-term contracts. This looks like a political non-starter, not least because what is good for heads is arguably just as good for teachers and administrators. But there is no reason to believe it would be good for heads or schools. Fixed contracts would encourage heads to play safe and avoid long-term change. American school superintendents contract for their services in this way, and often manage to float from one school board to another, making sure all the while of a stable base of political support.

Another suggestion is to take infinite pains over the procedure for choosing heads — or at least, more trouble than is often the case at present. Most heads and aspiring deputies have spine-chilling stories of the inanities and irrelevancies that have bulked large at interviewing panels, and to any head they have the ring of truth. There is scope for swifter administration, for a start: sometimes the best candidates have slipped away before the panel has agreed when to meet. Alternatively, it might be better to take more time over the job, and give the new incumbent a clear term between appointments in which he could undergo a pre-service course.

As for the selection procedure, there is a temptation to bring order to it by defining criteria by which the candidates shall be judged, defining the characteristics of the job in the particular school, and generally importing the apparatus of functionalism which has now gone out of fashion in industrial interviewing. The weakness of all this is that we have no satisfactory theory of either curriculum or its implementation: nor, for that matter, of management. Schwab (1969) has put the matter well:

> It is not a problem of selecting a representative of the appropriate personality type who exhibits the competences officially required for the job. The man we hire is more than a type and a bundle of competences. He is a multitude of probable behaviours which escape the net of personality theories and cognitive scales. He is endowed with prejudices, mannerisms, habits, tics, and relatives. And all of these manifold particulars will affect his work and the work of those who work for him. It is deliberation which operates in such cases to select the appropriate man.

A simpler way of preparing the panel for the task of selection would be to take steps to familiarise them with the school: its style, its aims, its problems. One would hope that the resigning head will have made it his business to bring the governing body in on more important matters than broken windows and blocked drains, and that as a result the governor members of the panel know at least something of its curriculum. And we can perhaps assume that the LEA officers will be well informed, since their advice will have been critical in drawing up the long and short lists. Ideally they will have spent a couple of days in the school to get the feel of it, and if the education committee representatives can be brought in as well for at least half a day, then so much the better. It simply will not do for any member of the panel to come to the interview as if he were buying another prize steer in the market. Detailed preparation is needed, and it is to do with people and their relationships rather than lists and prescriptions.

Finally, there is the suggestion that a staff college should be provided for heads under school regulations, just as for the armed services and civil service, and for senior staff in tertiary colleges and further education colleges. It is, indeed, a remarkable nonsense that the FE staff college is accessible to tertiary colleges, but not to sixth form colleges. But in any case, the argument for a coherent, central provision that could offer tailor-made courses for heads, before and after appointment, and a range of courses for senior staff in schools, is really overwhelming. If the Department of Education and Science cares that much about the quality of heads, then the local education authorities should take the initiative and call the department's bluff. The LEAs could agree to help finance the running costs, and guarantee to release newly-appointed heads for a pre-service course as well as existing heads for regular in-service courses: in return, the DES could provide the rest of the running costs and a suitable centre in which the college could be housed. (Local authorities in the North West jointly finance part-time courses for heads in a 'management centre': this is at least a beginning.)

The courses would offer basic advice on nuts-and-bolts matters, and introduce members to useful administrative techniques. College staff would forge links with management schools in higher education, and make use of general management approaches if they seemed relevant, and reliable. In the *Sunday Times* of 12.2.78, for example, James Poole describes a well-established residential course which deals with themes that are common to heads and business executives:

What working with rather than against others entails. If you are stuck try breaking your assumptions. Observe what you do well and build on that success. Groups need to know the why and how of anything before they can act. . . . Because the tasks are irrelevant and trivial, the training is in observing yourself and others cooperating.

While some approaches of this kind smack of fringe medicine, others could contribute much to the senior staff of schools. And, of course, the staff of the college would have a developmental function and would be able to devise new approaches which offer school-focused specificity.

The courses would deal, then, with performance skills in administration, and useful constructs in social science. But there is important work to be done which is distinctive to educational issues, and in particular, those that arise from the cultural and political context of whole-curriculum planning and implementation. Some topics for consideration have been suggested by Skilbeck (1972):

> First, studies in the management of group planning, including studies which focus on self-awareness and interpersonal relationships. Second, studies in systems analysis and strategic planning. . . . Third, studies in the politics of institutional life and of the distribution of power between the school and the wider environment. Fourth, studies in communication systems and particularly in the transformations undergone by values in the course of transmission. Fifth, studies in the cultural organisation of knowledge. . . .

If need were the criterion for providing a school staff college, it should have been done at the time of comprehensive reorganisation. But now that the contribution of a lively, well-informed, understanding head to curriculum innovation and implementation is supremely plain, and the observations of the Fookes Committee, in Parliament, have drawn attention to shortcomings in school performance, an ideal opportunity is presented to make a positive improvement to state education.

Schools and accountability

It is, of course, significant in itself that a parliamentary sub-committee should discuss education at some length, and it reflects the extent to which it has generally dawned that choices in education are social and political choices. Two conclusions follow from this. First, the basis for education decision-making must be wider than that of the purely professional arena: and second, schools may reasonably be expected to render public account of their activities. Neither of these is at all new. The structure of existing control mechanisms in English education, although not centralised, disperses power from national to local level, and assigns operational responsibility to local authorities as elected bodies, with a residual responsibility to the Secretary of State. And at school level, control of the curriculum is technically vested in the governors who also appoint staff, and to whom the head is part servant, part counsellor and part an independent executive, with a direct responsibility to the LEA and its officers. This diffused system involves widespread lay representation, and until recently has been generally regarded as adequately meeting the first requirement. Present dissatisfactions – of which the Taylor Committee is a symptom – spring from two sources. One is the growth of the parent-power lobby, and the other a widespread feeling that all is not as well as it might be with comprehensive schools. Each of these has deeper roots. Parent involvement is really an aspect of consumerism, which largely derives from forces to the left of the political centre; and educational dissatisfaction owes much to the anti-progressive movement of the political right, and which the Black Papers articulated in the early 1970s.

It is fair to say that schools and local authorities have often misjudged both influences. One might argue that LEA secondary transfer schemes which make parental choice the overriding criterion are an over-reaction, and the refusal of some heads even to publish a school prospectus rather the reverse. The trouble with parental choice, as the Secretary of State has discovered, is that one has a tiger by the tail; it is of note that the present chairman of the Society of Education Officers has pointed plainly to its harmful effects on the quality of educational provision, and this could be particularly serious as school rolls fall. And not only do parents lack information about schools: their choices tend to be based on subjective considerations which esteem the safe and familiar, and thus hamper curriculum innovation.

Errors of judgment have been made, too, by teachers' organisations, which have assumed since the war that the teacher's right to decide the curriculum is paramount. Until the 1978 constitution, the Schools Council's membership has been dominated by the teachers' organisations, and its policies (or, some might say, lack of them) have reflected this. Lawton (1977a) refers to inquiries made by the House of Commons Arts and Education Sub-Committee in 1976 of the Chairman and Joint Secretaries of the Council:

> Miss Janet Fookes, Chairman of the Sub-Committee, asked why the Council set such store by the teacher's right to fix the curriculum. She was told that it was because teachers were very strongly represented on the Council at all levels. One of the Joint Secretaries added that this was the result of a long tradition. The Sub-Committee did not seem entirely convinced by the argument that teachers' autonomy was the supreme criterion when discussing curriculum change.

In fact, as Lawton points out, the tradition goes back no further than the 1944 Act, which left curriculum content unspecified, and the General Certificate of Education of 1950 which left schools free to enter pupils for whatever subjects they wished.

The importance of examinations is that they largely fulfil the second requirement we have drawn from the essentially political basis of educational decisions: that schools should be publicly accountable for what they do. For many heads, announcing the GCE results and university places at the annual speech day is a necessary and sufficient way of letting parents know that all is well. The LEA is satisfied that the school is competently run: the governors have dismissed no staff, and suspended few pupils. What more can the concept of accountability mean?

This is a question of central importance in curriculum innovation. For one thing, innovation may mean new styles of learning, and new styles of examination to test them. Yet the acceptance by employers of the CSE examination has been disappointing, and so parents will regard new developments with suspicion. But who should decide on these developments? How can their success be judged? We can see that the underlying issue is that of control, and it is linked with the question of evaluation. Can we – ought we – to rely on teachers to fix the curriculum, and on their capacity to judge its effects? What are the rights in the matter of parents, ratepayers and Parliament – and, too, of pupils?

We can see that both consumerism and anti-progressivism are really to do with accountability, and it has been noted that they draw strength from a wide political spectrum. (One might add, for example, that while education vouchers have, in the UK, attracted the support of right-wingers, in the US it is the left who have supported them.) What has brought the issue to the fore has been the adverse economic climate since 1974. Education is a big spender, and accountability implies responsibility. Voters are keen to know how responsibly the education service uses its funds, and the climate of doubt already existed. The seeming reluctance of schools to open their doors – if not their books – and educate parents as well as pupils can hardly have helped. The result has been political intervention, and much myth-making about school practice and performance. The 'great debate' was both a safety valve, and a reminder to the schools that education can never be a private preserve.

We can be entirely hopeful about these developments. They offer the prospect of a partnership between school and community which can lead directly to whole-curriculum planning. We should note that the 1978 HMI document *Curriculum 11–16* prefaces its recipe for a common curriculum with the question: 'What do pupils have a right to expect if they are obliged to stay in schools until they are 16?' The pupil's right to a good education leads, we may argue, to a rationale for a common curriculum based on a selection from the culture, and which should quite properly stem from a process of deliberation involving parents and the wider community of employers and local interests. But its underpinning rationale will derive from educational considerations, and the professional expertise, in these matters, of head and staff will not be in dispute. The task of schools is to ensure that they are familiar with the kinds of judgments such a process involves, and are ready to establish the necessary consultative procedures to ensure that the implementation of a common curriculum can proceed on a secure base.

We have seen, though, some adverse side effects of the public agony that has brought the accountability issue to the fore, and doubtless there will be others. An important task for heads and educationists is to monitor these developments and use their community role to provoke discussion and, if necessary, action. For example, the light-sampling techniques of the Assessment of Performance Unit (APU) at the DES might have only a small backwash effect on the curriculum, take up but little school time, and provide useful information: but let there be no doubt that they will have some curriculum effect. And it seems likely that by the time the results have been digested and made available, years will have passed and circumstances changed. The APU testing will consume substantial funds, and could easily have an inhibiting effect on curriculum development with little useful information in return. They are a purely political development, which might have been avoided if the interests of teachers and schools had been more skilfully represented in the political arena. Now we are stuck with them, and all we can do is make the best of a bad job.

A particular danger is that LEAs will go beyond the APU light-sampling concept, and see testing as the kind of accountability approach that would appeal to some local politicians. This brings us to our last topic, which is that of evaluating the effects of an educational programme. And the first thing we must say is that no one knows, in a general sense, how to evaluate in education. This is probably why evaluation has become the latest growth industry in the curriculum field. The call for accountability — whether to justify a new curriculum project, or a state-wide education system — offers rich pickings to those who can offer acceptable schemes. And this leads to our second point: that judging educational decisions is just as political and social a process as making them, and so we cannot escape from subjective judgments and find the curriculum equivalent of absolute zero. The best we can ever do is assess the basis of the evaluation, and decide whether it is defensible within our own frame of reference.

Curriculum and evaluation

The position, then, in the evaluation field is that administrators and politicians are looking for systems of assessment in a field where no objective judgments exist. It is precisely analogous to the function of criticism in modern art, and — as Tom Wolfe has wittily pointed out — the key element here is not whether a painting is enriching or valuable, but whether it is supported by a persuasive theory. The hollow centre at the core of the judgmental process is filled not by *a priori* attempts to see it against an aesthetic background that acknowledges difficulties and justifies assumptions, but by a theory of art criticism chosen from those that are currently fashionable. Wolfe's comments on theories of art criticism (1976) could well describe the logic-chopping analysis and stylised writing which characterises much of the work of the 'new wave' evaluators in education:

> But the theories, I insist, were *beautiful*. Theories? They were more than theories, they were mental constructs. No, more than that even . . . veritable edifices behind the eyeballs they were . . . castles in the cortex . . . mezuzahs on the pyramids of Betz . . . crystalline . . . comparable in their bizarre refinements to mediaeval Scholasticism.

It is necessary, though, to know something of these developments. First, because the innovating school must come to terms with the need to evaluate, and therefore make decisions about how it should be done: and second, because the language-game of evaluation gets fed back into the curriculum development system, and if we are being influenced, it is as well to know what is doing the influencing.

In this brief account, we need to note two fundamental issues. It is essential first to be clear about means and ends in education, if only because our political masters might readily assume that schools and projects have well-defined ends that can be agreed in advance, and measured in retrospect: and so can be evaluated and rendered accountable at both ends of the process. A series of achievement tests in between will then provide complete control.

It is certainly necessary, as I have argued in the last chapter, to plan the curriculum with an awareness of outcomes and objectives, and 'the characterisation of such ends is logically prior to the means . . . . The items of knowledge we want, the attitudes, values, skills, habits and so on' (Hirst, 1973). It follows that educators should undertake the task of indicating in advance what they hope to achieve, and will need a rational way of justifying those hopes. It is true, too, that it will then be possible to say something definite about the means that will be required. But it does not follow that the ends will take some measurable form. This may be possible in some cases: examinations, for example, are reasonably reliable tests of factual recall. But their reliability rests on subjective procedures; it is significant that the APU proposals for mathematics and science tests have attracted much criticism from examination boards and professional associations. And it would be difficult to devise a satisfactory examination that would test a pupil's ability to, say, work well with another on a common task. I have no doubt that behavioural scientists could produce one: but I doubt whether it would carry conviction. And it would, of course, be impossible to verify in any objective sense. We may therefore conclude that attempts to measure educational success by the use of behavioural objectives are unlikely to offer more than a partial answer to the problem.

There is the further point that while we shall be aware of the outcomes we have in mind, it would be wrong to regard them so inflexibly that the means cannot modify the ends. Education is not a prescriptive, feed-forward process, like the styles of bureaucratic management to which the techniques of Management by Objectives (MBO) or Planned Programme Budgeting Systems (PPBS) seem to lend themselves. It is to do with cognitive changes in human beings, and so our means-end model will take what MacDonald-Ross (1975) has called 'the expedient route, which uses the information about means to restrict the goals that are aimed for'. It is a route which

is closer to the traditional evolution, for it stresses feed-back, successive adjustment, cyclic procedures of design. It is the standard mode for the political animal, and has been called 'the art of the possible' . . . .

A trivial example might make the point clear. In the card game of Rummy, the end is clearly stated: to arrange one's cards in given sequences. The means is equally clear: a card may be picked up and another discarded at each turn. If the player adopted a rigid concept of a means-end model, he would determine from his original hand what sequences he would aim for, and depend on luck to provide the right cards. But he would be unlikely to beat the player who noted the sequences laid down during the game by the other players, and used this information not only to modify his original aims, but also to fit odd cards where possible into these sequences. In short, the skilful player is aware of desired outcomes, and modifies his interpretation of them in the light of the game's process.

The second fundamental issue in evaluation is of a different kind, but has a connection with our discussion of means and ends. It seems as if two camps have sprung up in educational research and evaluation. There are those who, in our present context, would argue that we can, and must, specify measurable outcomes: and those who would maintain that this is entirely impossible, and only a variety of descriptive techniques can be satisfactory. The dichotomy has been described by Gibson (1978):

> The problem is that there has been a polarisation of beliefs: beliefs about what constitutes truth, and about what constitutes appropriate methods of discovering and recording that truth. This polarisation may be identified as on the one hand the dogma of positivism and, on the other, the dogma of interpretation (or the counter-tradition).. . . A wide range of labels identifies the two positions: objectivity *versus* subjectivity; . . . empiricism *versus* understanding; the natural sciences *versus* the human or social sciences.

Dangers arise when either position becomes a matter of dogmatism, so that the two traditions are in conflict rather than complementing each other. Within the social sciences a sharp conflict between the empirical, classifying approach (evident, for example, in systems analysis) and the pragmatic, relativist approach is evident in many fields; and it can be identified in styles of curriculum design and of the analysis of curriculum change. We shall see that it has had an important influence in evaluation too.

Curriculum evaluation began as an offshoot of the American research-development-diffusion projects. These were usually concerned with up-dating subject content, with outcomes in measurable form. This made the experimental or psychometric approach an obvious choice. The results of achievement tests could be compared with the performance of a control group, and treated as the yield of the experiment just as, between the wars, statistical techniques were developed for comparing the yields from crops grown under varying conditions. This form of evaluation has been said to exhibit, therefore, the 'agricultural-botany paradigm' (Hamilton, 1976). A British example is the initial teaching alphabet experiment, launched in the early 1960s. The results were inconclusive, because of the effects of variables – for instance, the influence of teachers – which are not susceptible to control. Because the objectives of the project are stated in advance, and the evaluation is carried out at the end, it is said to be both pre-ordinate and summative.

A way of eliminating control and comparison problems was to make the project itself define the objective. Then all that is necessary is to test the end result, and see how far this indicates achievement of the objective. This, though, implies a rigid means-end model, and the use of so-called behavioural objectives, which specify outcomes in terms of changes in observed patterns of behaviour. The evaluator joins the project team from the beginning, and the evaluation is concurrent with the project. It is said to be formative rather than summative.

The main difficulty is in specifying, and justifying, the outcomes in the appropriate form. Research shows that teachers do not work in this way: for example, Hamilton remarks that Scottish science teachers wanted a prime objective of the Scottish Integrated Science Scheme to be that 'Pupils should acquire interest and enthusiasm for science'. This is reasonable enough; but it is not a suitable objective for a behavioural means-end project. Another difficulty with having a living-in evaluator is that the research design becomes paramount. Teachers involved in the Swedish IMU Individualised Mathematics Programme, for example, were forbidden to make what they saw as desirable changes to the teaching arrangements for fear of upsetting the evaluation schedule.

A critique of the behavioural or objectives model has been given by Stenhouse (1975). Perhaps its most serious drawback is the static, almost demeaning view it implies of the role of the teacher:

> The objectives model applied to knowledge areas seems to me to concentrate on improving teaching as instruction without increment to the wisdom or scholarship of the teacher. . . . It is a means of bettering students' performance without improving teachers' personal and professional quality.

We have seen that in a common-culture curriculum, teachers are involved in a dynamic process of selecting knowledge and monitoring their efforts. And in any event, the very specificity of the objectives model makes it difficult to see how it can be projected beyond subject-based frames of reference to the interrelated whole curriculum. But in rejecting this model and its associated style of evaluation, we must be careful to remember that we are not rejecting the notion of objectives in toto: merely the behavioural way of defining them and treating them which is generally known as the 'objectives model'. I have taken pains to stress that prior knowledge of ends will be logical and necessary. Also, it would be wrong to associate psychometric methods of evaluation exclusively with the objectives model: we must think twice before rejecting any technique which might be of help in assessing the learning process.

By the end of the 1960s, there was a pronounced swing away from RDD models of curriculum change, as we have seen, towards diffusion and problem-solving strategies. There was a parallel shift in thinking about evaluation: in fact, curriculum development and curriculum evaluation are simply two sides of the same coin. The 'new wave' evaluators rejected the technocratic emphasis on empirical analysis in favour of description and understanding – the alternative model of belief-system. This echoed, too, the interest of the sociologists of education in self-understanding rather than external causes, and curriculum as a historically-determined phenomenon. The relevant disciplines for the new evaluators were not psychology and statistics, but sociology, anthropology and history. The new aim was to be not formal and precise, but responsive, illuminative, relevant and accessible. Whereas the experimental evaluator, like the scientist, asks − what are the measurable effects of carrying out this new procedure? − the illuminative evaluator 'makes few direct comments on the effects of an innovation. In general, his concern is more with the context and process of innovation than with outcomes' (Munro, 1977). MacDonald (1973) has made the point tellingly:

> The impact of an innovation is not a set of discrete effects, but an organically related pattern of acts and consequences. To understand fully a single act, one must locate it functionally within that pattern. . . . Innovations have many more unanticipated consequences than is normally assumed in development and evaluation design.

One has only to think of some of the impoverished designs which pass for research into classroom teaching styles and mixed-ability grouping to realise how rarely MacDonald's observation is heeded, and how misleading a restricted concept of evaluation can be.

The new, illuminative approach has developed its own jargon, and its own quasi-theological questions, as this passage from Hamilton (1976) suggests:

> Flexible, 'goal-free' evaluations that are 'responsive' to the 'transactional' relationship between evaluator, client and audience have developed to replace 'goal-based', 'preordinate' studies that rely simply on the logic of an imported and largely alien technology. By adopting a stance of cultural pluralism . . . evaluation has moved into new territory. It has relinquished the security of objective, universally agreed criteria . . . the technological question, 'Which criteria?' becomes a social question, 'Whose criteria?' Where does this lead the evaluator?

Well, if the evaluator is to take a polarised view and see goal-free or illuminative evaluation as uniquely *replacing* goal-based approaches, he will fall into the same trap as the researcher who ignores the historical context because he sees it as unscientific, or the curriculum developer who argues that the teacher can do without educational ends and purposes. For the two traditions have much to offer each other; we have examined this in some detail in the case of curriculum models, and it is equally true for evaluation models. For while the experimental model suffers from the defects we have mentioned, the illuminative model is under- rather than over-specified. It might easily amount to little more than a kind of anecdotal *reportage*. And if it becomes the exclusive property of a private in-group or *cenacle* (to use Wolfe's word), it will become more rather than less remote to teachers.

Although one might easily gain the contrary impression, there is no reason why the two styles should be incompatible. That they are often portrayed as such is an indication of the generally immature and pre-theoretic state of the curriculum field. As Munro puts it:

> However, whereas the experimenter may indeed forget the 'humanness' of his study, the illuminator, because of the scope of his concern, may produce such diffuse (or even distorted) comment that it cannot be usefully tested or used as a guide to improved action.

And in any case, do we really need a separate breed of evaluators? As Jenkins (1977) remarks, summarising a discussion on evaluation involving evaluators, developers and teachers: 'Does evaluation have to be big-science? Why can't schools build up from the informal evaluations they already practise?' Such approaches have several attractions. Perhaps most important is that while distinctions between curriculum design, implementation and evaluation have a heuristic value, the more unity that can be brought to the process of curriculum development the more likely it is to succeed. The innovating school is its own unifying framework. And if the teacher operates by having in mind desired outcomes of the learning process, then it is reasonable to suppose that he will bring a set of criteria to bear on the ultimate outcomes and thus evaluate his effectiveness and the pupil's learning. Stenhouse (1975) takes this view, and goes on to see the teacher as researcher:

> The idea is that of an educational science in which each classroom is a laboratory, each teacher a member of the scientific community . . . a curriculum is a means of studying the problems and effects of implementing any defined line of teaching.

There seems to me to be a danger that such a role for the teacher might become rather self-involved and solipsistic. Apart from the feeling that the methods of scientific research are not cognate with the often intuitive skills of the teacher, too much 'systematic questioning of one's own teaching as a basis for development' might be too much of a good thing. It was W. C. Fields, recalling his early days as a conjurer, who remarked that if he had ever stopped to wonder how he did it, he would never have been able to do it again. Certainly 'know thyself' is a motto for every teacher; but it is a creative activity too, and there is an instinctive link between intention and action which involves a non-analytic style of thinking. I have suggested elsewhere (Holt, 1978) that a 'creative action' model of teaching can achieve the sought-after unity without implying a research paradigm. More important, it allows the teacher to see his role in conjunction with that of other teachers; the 'defined line of teaching' is not just the result of his own interaction with the learner, but also takes account of the agreed curriculum strategies of the faculty and of the school.

The growth of interest in school-based curriculum development gives these questions a new importance, and we can readily see that preordinate styles of evaluation will not, in their classically pure form, be appropriate for adjudicating a process which allows its means to influence its ends. A number of illuminative evaluation models have therefore been devised which, on the face of it, are much better suited to school-based applications. The 'countenance' model of Stake (1967) aims to give a broad picture of the curriculum, and report the ways different people see it. The role of teachers is to keep records of their work and offer their opinions. The task of the evaluator is to collect judgments rather than make them. The 'SAFARI' study supported at Norwich by the Ford Foundation is an expression of the 'teacher as researcher' philosophy, and sees evaluation as a case-study exercise in which the accuracy and fairness of the researchers' reports is 'democratically' negotiated with the teachers. But as Jenkins (1977) remarks:

> The more a case study of an individual school approximates to self-description . . . the more difficult becomes the task of generalising from the *instance* to the *class*. Indeed the SAFARI exercise is held by some to be producing formative evaluations of individual schools under the guise of summative evaluations of national projects.

There is a vagueness about these approaches which leads one back to a model based on the innovating school itself. Such a one is the 'institutional self-study model' developed (like Stake's) in America and which aims 'to review content and procedures of instruction' (Jenkins, 1976). Staff involvement takes the form of committee discussions, and there is the possibility of 'outside authentication or technical help'. My own experience of school-based innovation suggests that this is on the right lines, providing it is carried out eclectically rather than dogmatically. There is a variety of ways in which teachers, parents and administrators can justifiably form opinions on a school's work, and the innovating school should be sensitive to all those that can be defended rationally. And in a commonsense way, schools can make use of outside help and advice without losing too much sleep about the niceties of 'value-pluralism' and 'democratic negotiation'. At the moment such help is not readily available. In the next chapters we shall consider the nature of present provision and the extent to which it might be modified and enlarged.

This discussion of evaluation has taken us on a route which has, in a sense, led us through some prepared positions and out the other side. But it has helped us to clarify our understanding of the political and educational strengths of the school that is engaged upon a programme of cultural synthesis, and shown that system-based curriculum development means school-based evaluation, as well as school-based design and implementation. There is nothing very surprising in this: it shows that the position is self-consistent, and that what must begin with the teacher must also end with him. It is the rationale of the curriculum which provides the vital reference point both with the school's community, and with national and regional criteria of educational aims and performance.

We can end as we began — with an acknowledgment that in helping the head to develop appropriate leadership styles, and teachers to pursue understanding and implement outcomes, what ultimately matters is the framework of human relations and intentions that defines and inspires the school's curriculum programme. Recipes and prescriptions are not to be despised: we cannot depend on simply muddling through. But alone, they are not enough. Perhaps the last word should go to Mr Venus who, in *Our Mutual Friend*, is asked for the recipe for cobbler's punch:

> It's difficult to impart . . . because, however particular you may be in allotting your materials, so much will still depend upon the individual gifts, and there being a feeling thrown into it.

Chapter 5

Agencies for Change

The theme of 'only connect' is bound to find a central place in any view of education which stresses the breadth of our culture and the importance of human factors in the collaborative enterprises which will define and sustain the programmes that can implement this breadth. The teacher will connect with other teachers, from both within and outside his subject specialism: the events of the classroom will need a more collegial perspective. The head will connect with the staff by a pattern of delegation and interaction that depends less on authority and more on function. And the school – as the corporate expression of these professional activities – will make cultural, administrative and academic connections with a wider community, as well as its local one. These two-way transactions will nourish the individuality of both teacher and school, and help to change attitudes as well as transmit policies.

Up to now, the main focus of our attention has been the nature of the regeneration process in the school itself. But we have noted that the national project, social diffusion and problem-solving modes of development all involve the school, to a varying extent, in an engagement with agencies that lie outside it. We need now to look at these agencies and the job they do, and consider how they might change so as to facilitate innovation when a school is developing a common-culture curriculum.

The external influences on the school might have any or all of four distinct functions. They might be part of the mechanism of political control; have an innovative purpose; form part of in-service education; or represent a form of evaluation. And these functions might be explicit or implicit: thus the governors' decision that German should not be the first foreign language is explicit, while the influence of the GCE examiners, or university subject departments, on the curriculum in main school and sixth form is implicit. Between these states lie the recommendations of advisers and inspectors which the head will need at least to consider, if not respond to. Overlaps of this kind are inevitable in a system that deals in complex issues, yet recognises the value of pluralism both nationally and locally. It follows that not only are the functions of some agencies likely to show signs of mutual conflict; prescribing new roles or new agencies is a hazardous business, and needs to take account of what is possible and not merely desirable.

Her Majesty's Inspectorate

Historically, the oldest of these agencies is Her Majesty's Inspectorate, and the 1840 Instructions to H.M. Inspectors state (Maclure, 1965):

> this inspection is not intended as a means of exercising control, but of affording assistance. . . . It is not to be regarded as operating for the restraint of local efforts, but for their encouragement. . . . The Inspector having no power to interfere, and not being instructed to offer any advice or information excepting where it is invited.

But the HMI role is essentially political — they are, after all, directly responsible to the Secretary of State, although the career civil servants have largely wriggled in between — and it was probably no coincidence that during the 1960s, when teacher autonomy reached its tactical zenith, the emphasis moved back to assistance and away from inspection, after moving the other way between the wars when the Regulations of the Board of Education determined the curriculum, and HMI made sure that this was what happened. This withdrawal into an advisory role made them marginal men at a time when a more explicit role might have made for a greater resolution of educational purpose as comprehensive reorganisation got under way. But the Department of Education and Science was equally reluctant to declare itself, and so such advice as HMI offered remained confined to familiar subject-based grooves. An opportunity, though, for HMI to play a larger part arose right at the beginning of the decade, when the Minister, David (now Lord) Eccles, proposed in 1960 the formation of the Curriculum Study Group. It is generally considered that the CSG, founded in 1962 and dead by 1964, was a victim of the joint dislike of Sir Ronald Gould, representing the National Union of Teachers, and William (now Lord) Alexander, representing the Association of Education Committees. But in a conversation reported by Devlin and Warnock (1977), Lord Eccles puts a different slant on events:

> Lord Eccles told us in January 1977: 'I wanted the HMIs taken out of the building and made into a think-tank, a research and development unit, to help the Minister.' He recalled that his group failed principally because the inspectors themselves were not enthusiastic. ('They had too much liking for being big people when they went round schools.')

The indications now, however, are that the changed political mood will to some extent thrust a more aggressive role upon the Inspectorate. More interventionist, at any rate: for the first time in years, HMI are standing up and being counted, sometimes with a loud Report, like the recent *Curriculum 11—16* document. Ever more forthright papers trickle out of Elizabeth House, each with its inevitable policy disclaimer, its more or less rotund prose, and its curious mixture of the aloof with the anecdotal. The quality is variable, as one would expect from people who are intelligent but overworked, in the centre of things and yet in no way part of them. Some documents, like that on gifted children (Matters for Discussion 4: 1977, HMSO) are sensible and perceptive, cutting through prejudice and assumption in an area where a measure of detachment from local pressures and national politics can only be helpful: others, like its predecessor on modern languages (No. 3) seem to offer opinions with the confidence only accessible to those who have second-hand knowledge to go on.

But the directive strength of the Inspectorate is considerable. It acts on schools in three ways. First, there is the immediacy of the HMI in the school, paying a visit either alone or as part of a team. In general, these visits are too short to be of much good, and they are probably as unsatisfactory for the HMI as for the head. They will work best when the HMI can offer sound advice in his particular field, putting the school at once in touch with useful theory and good practice. I heard a senior HMI assure a meeting of secondary heads recently that illuminative evaluation was really what they were about; but this is to imply taking time to discover the school's intentions, and present them in some generally useful way. Perhaps this occurs now and again when a team can work in a school for a period of weeks, but there is another snag: how detached can an HMI ever be from his control function? To some teachers, he may appear a counsellor; to others, a *voyeur*; and to others, an agent of the secret police. The terrible truth is probably that the role itself makes school contacts the least satisfactory part of the job.

The second way in which the Inspectorate influences schools is through contacts with LEAs. There seems to be no available study of this process, which is a pity: we can only make an inspired guess. But the links here will be with the chief and deputy education officers, and senior advisers; and they will influence the climate of thought and action which will eventually manifest itself in in-service courses with a particular emphasis, or development grants available for a specific purpose: or perhaps even some explicit line of policy. The CEO of at least one of the county authorities currently involved in the HMI pilot study of curriculum development in trial schools along the lines of the *Curriculum 11–16* document, for instance, has publicly stated his enthusiasm for this departure and his authority's commitment to it. (He is, interestingly enough, a former HMI.)

Finally, there are the public opportunities given to HMI to state their views at meetings and lectures. Some seem to regard this sort of activity with much diffidence, and look uncomfortable even on the back row: others – usually the more senior ones – can display an engaging informality. In either case, their opinions will be noted and pondered over, and this will be particularly the case when teachers attend a DES course run by the Inspectorate. Yet how directly influential these courses are in changing attitudes in teachers, and actual practice in schools, is problematic. If you were to pick up the booklet that lists all these courses and study their titles, and know how oversubscribed they are, and how hand-picked the staff are, you might think that in no time at all, the organisation and management of schools or the teaching of modern mathematics would attain perfection up and down the country. But the booklet was just as impressive five years ago, and ten years ago; and very little has really changed.

Local education authorities

In-service courses of this sort are, though, of uncertain effectiveness, whoever runs them. On the whole, it seems likely that the influence of the Inspectorate is a factor which gains greatly in potency when it acts in combination with other factors, and this leads us to a consideration of the involvement of LEAs in curriculum change.

While all local authorities must accept responsibility for the education in their schools, it can be done with a light or heavy touch depending on the interest of the elected members and the inclinations of the senior officers who serve them. Any distinct change in the party-political complexion of the authority is almost certain to be felt in the schools: partly because the education bill is a big one, and so a prime target for cuts; and partly because the demise of Butskellism on the national scene has made education a party issue. We have moved a long way from the central ground of the early 1960s, when Crosland and Boyle, although education ministers in opposing administrations, could speak in the same terms of comprehensive education, and the ability of children to acquire intelligence. Even as late as 1970, a Conservative leader (Heath) could declare that the separation of GCE O-level and CSE at 16-plus was undesirable, and that a common examination system should be encouraged. The 1977 decision of a Labour education secretary (Williams) not to accept the Schools

Council's proposal for such a system, but rather to refer it to a special committee for consideration on technical grounds, is a measure of the wariness with which politicians in both parties now approach issues which were hitherto far from contentious. (The subsequent adoption of this proposal in modified form in the 1978 White Paper, following the report of the Waddell Committee, is discussed in chapter 6.) On the local scene, therefore, political action could take a variety of forms, ranging from staffing cuts or the withdrawal of assisted places for independent schools to a greater emphasis on selection between schools or within them.

For the officers of the authority, the principal effect of all this political activity is to take up time which would otherwise be available to improve the service provided. And the adoption of corporate management, following local government reorganisation, hasn't helped: the education department might be the last to hear, in some authorities, about changes in, say, ancillary staff establishments which could profoundly affect schools: the needs of the education service are quite different from those of hospitals or leisure centres, but its officers may need to fight every inch of the way in order to ensure adequate consultation. In the past, a CEO might well consider that the appointment of a secondary head was of the first importance, and give the selection procedures and the final interview his personal attention. He is now almost certain to delegate the whole operation, and even his attendance at the appointment might be sacrificed in favour of a key finance committee meeting. The atmosphere of uncertainty makes long-term planning seem rather reckless, and generates a climate in which educational ideas wilt, and the bureaucratic vegetation of committees and sub-committees, working papers and minutes, feasibility proposals and references back grows ever more luxuriant. It is an atmosphere of suspicion and possibly pettiness: very different from the reconstructionist mood which saw the innovations of Newsom in Hertfordshire, Clegg in the West Riding and Mason in Leicestershire. *The Times* obituary of John Newsom (24.5.71), who was appointed CEO in 1940 at the age of 30 with negligible previous educational experience, shows how much things have changed:

> He was a brilliant and unorthodox administrator. Not by any means an administrator's administrator, his achievements lay in the field of altering attitudes and creating the circumstances in which good education could flourish by releasing initiative in others.

The buccaneers and ideas-men have given way to the sobersides of the committee room, and at a time of rapid social and economic change, the climate for innovation is perhaps more inhibiting than ever.

Local authority advisers and inspectors

It is against this background that we must judge the work of LEA advisers, whose numbers have grown substantially during the 1960s. Their national association recommends one adviser for every 20,000 of the total population, but only three of the LEAs sampled in a recent study reached this figure. This useful research (Bolam, Smith and Canter, 1976) was financed by the DES, and indicates to an extent the amount of information sought and absorbed by that body. It is the only up-to-date study in this field, and I am indebted to it for the facts referred to below.

Most advisers have a specific subject responsibility, but some have a general responsibility for a sector of the service (area or level advisers) or for organising other advisers. But less than a third of advisers, of both sorts, wanted to spend more time evaluating the performance of teachers and probationers, and 'very few related the issue of assessment to the fundamental and wider task of supporting teachers' career development'. Most visits to schools were of one to three hours' duration, and over 80 per cent were special purpose visits of one kind or another. Of these,

> twice as many were concerned with personnel matters as were concerned with advising on classroom teaching, and on one third of the total visits described the adviser did not meet any teaching staff employed at the school at all apart from the headteacher.

125

A high proportion wanted to spend less time on administrative work, and over half on the indirect reporting of their work to education officers rather than the committees for whom the reports were intended. In fact,

> a great deal of criticism was directed at the role of administrators in transmitting advice and indeed the whole relationship of advisers and administrators came in for criticism too.

Bolam, Smith and Canter were especially concerned with the role of the advisers in promoting innovation. But at least a third of the sample were unable, for whatever reason, 'to carry out the kind of innovative role they preferred', and it was the subject advisers who were most likely to see themselves as innovators. A major difficulty is the detached nature of the job:

> Advisers were external to the schools by reason of their institutional base, external to the power structure of the LEA by reason of its hierarchy and even, by reason of their subject specialisation, cut off from other members of the team with whom they shared office accommodation
> . . .

Of particular interest are the results of asking advisers which, of 13 key innovation strategies, were most relevant to their work. The highest ratings went to in-service training and proposing solutions to schools based on the adviser's diagnosis of the problem: the lowest to 'helping schools to devise their own problem-solving procedures and to giving feedback to research and development projects'. While advisers are interested in curriculum development, it appears that they see it from the point of view of the supplier rather than the user. What is expressly lacking is an involvement in the management of curriculum change. A survey by Townsend (1970) throws light on the nature of the adviser's INSET role: it appears that LEAs – that is, advisers – organised nearly 60 per cent of the total courses attended by teachers, and almost all of these were of 14 days or less in length. And the courses were more popular with primary and women teachers than with men and secondary teachers.

Two case studies carried out by Bolam, Smith and Canter suggested that advisers are unlikely to carry their interest in an evaluation beyond the initiation stage, or to make use of relevant research and theoretical literature. There is evidence that advisers tend to spend time in favourite schools, and have little contact with agencies like the Schools Council. A central problem is that, like the god Janus, they face two ways:

> They are required to face in two directions simultaneously — towards the teachers and schools and towards the policy makers and administrators. At worst, this can mean that both teachers and administrators regard inspectors [advisers] as marginal figures who offer idealistic solutions to problems that are not their central concern.

The difficulty of defining a clear role extends to those authorities who have organised their advisers into teams, usually under a chief adviser. It is not clear how team policy is formulated, or how their procedures are monitored within the team.

Three phases of curriculum change

Let us look back on the work of HM Inspectors and LEA advisers or inspectors (the two terms are to a large extent interchangeable), and see what general conclusions we can draw. It is clear that both exhibit Janus characteristics, because their two functions serve different ends which may well conflict. The 1840 distinction between control and assistance holds good: control associates them with aims and criteria developed outside the school, and might be power-coercive, inspectorial and bureaucratic — certainly evaluative and administrative. Assistance associates them with aims and criteria developed inside the school, and might range from counselling individual teachers to nursing the installation of some major project.

We can see at once that there will be reinforcement of these ends or role-dimensions when teachers and schools move in lock-step with local or national guidelines. When the content of the curriculum was regulated during the first half of this century, knowledge fields were reasonably stable and pluralism in society's values was reasonably absent. The interests of teacher and administrator met in the subject classroom and the subject examination syllabus. Curriculum development was synonymous with examination revision, and the Inspectorate could publish its recommendations on subject teaching in the confidence that the only obstacle to their adoption would be the natural inertia of the body educational. In effect, there was no dispute about what should be taught, or how to do it. HMI and advisers could sleep easily in their beds, free from role-induced insecurity or loss of identity.

In this first, uncomplicated phase, curriculum change was essentially haphazard and not notably innovatory. It has been likened to routine maintenance: modifying subject content and method, providing refresher courses, introducing new syllabuses or better textbooks. Unplanned, non-innovatory, subject-based change offered autonomy to schools and no threat to centralist intentions.

The second phase was inevitable as soon as the curriculum became undefined. But its advance was hastened by new technological visions in the 1960s, and the advent of cafeteria-style subject projects which reflected the new article of faith: schools should be free to do what they fancy. Change was still subject-based, like the curriculum, and still unplanned: but it did involve genuine innovation. How did inspectors and advisers respond? Well, two further factors kept their hands full: there was comprehensive reorganisation, and a huge expansion in the teaching force to meet a rising school population. Existing teachers had to be helped to tackle different ranges of ability, and new teachers meant college courses to establish and probationary years to monitor. And even if there had been time to examine the shape of the emergent multiple-choice curriculum, no one seemed anxious to do it. Certainly the politicians had no stomach for it, and so the DES had only an attenuated control function to exercise. The Inspectorate inspected less, and was pleased to say so; HMI emerged as a kind of ruminant animal, chewing over the piecemeal adoption of non-streaming, or Nuffield French, or Project Technology, and taking as their judgmental base line – in the absence of any public criteria outside the exam room — their assessment of the extent and quality of learning across the ability range. This muted, personalised kind of control packed little stopping power: if it irritated, it was because the new projects seemed to their exponents to be good in themselves.

For local authority advisers, subject projects suited perfectly a role as conveyor to the schools of things bright and beautiful; for the essence, as we have noted, of these projects was the assumption that once the project team had devised and trialled the materials, dissemination would do the rest. As the developers placed more emphasis on social interaction, teachers' centres were seen as a way of sustaining local groups: this confirms the picture of advisers as Santa Claus figures who help push the goodies down the chimney, but who rarely take part in the subsequent fun and games other than at first remove — by running courses, not by joining in. And teachers' centres are still external to the school: little wonder that Owen might ask, in 1973:

> It is within these centres that the main impetus of management is expected nowadays to reside. Those who are Wardens of these centres . . . are the managers. Do they have a proper job to do? Do they know how to manage change?

That his doubts were justified was confirmed by Rudduck in 1976, reporting on the role of teachers' centre leaders in the dissemination of the Humanities Curriculum Project:

> We were often aware of the limited power of the leaders: they were generally unable to take initiatives that had financial implications and their activities were sometimes inhibited by problems of status. . . . We detected some evidence of conflict between advisory staff and full-time teachers' centre leaders. It made us ask what was the distinctive role of the adviser in curriculum development. Is he to initiate and supervise curriculum change in close . . . contact with the decision-makers in the schools, or is he to respond to initiatives by organising a support superstructure . . .?

The answer would seem to be, a bit of both: he can help

initiate, but rarely supervise; and he can offer a course-based response, but it will fit the schools — and the teachers' centres — only where it touches. But we have the advantage of hindsight, and are getting ahead of ourselves. The point to note is that during this second phase of development, role-conflict problems for advisers were not in the schools, but outside them: national projects had helped generate new kinds of external agencies which muddied the waters lapping round the schools, but not in them. And if advisers exerted any control function in the schools, it was a carrot, not a stick: extra tape recorders if this project were adopted, a new class-sized greenhouse if environmental studies got a bigger lick of the option spoon. The basic conflict still lay hidden beneath the surface.

If the first phase was one of traditional development, taking us to 1960, then the second was one of piecemeal development and lasted until quite recently. The third phase is of system development, and it is just beginning. With this time scale, the Bolam, Smith and Canter study chronicles the tensions emerging during the end of the second phase, as the problems of the new loom larger. To say it is well timed is simply to acknowledge that the commissioning of such a study is itself a response to changing conditions. And the change is a fundamental one: society seems to have made up its mind about the curriculum, and a group of HMIs can now write (*Curriculum 11–16*, 1978):

> A major obstacle to coherent development is . . . a deep reluctance to face the implications of partnership in curriculum planning. . . . It is doubtful if the country can afford — educationally as well as financially — the wasted effort, experiments embarked upon and left unfinished or unexamined, unnecessary repetitions, and, most of all, the apparent lack of agreement on fundamental objectives. Indeed, all this is freely acknowledged in discussions all over the country by heads, teachers and administrators.

And it is all true: for fifteen years, the Inspectorate has sat on its hands and charted the wreckage of a voyage of disorder. Yet some have suggested that HMI should leave the curriculum alone, and inspect it rather than philosophise about it. The whole point is that unless they think about the curriculum, they cannot suggest what it should look like: and unless they make such suggestions, they cannot inspect – that is, control – it. Furthermore, it is infinitely better for the health of schools that these matters should be publicly aired, so that they can be challenged and argued over, rather than swept discreetly under the carpet on the assumption that some sort of consensus exists.

This brings us to a further point. The above extract suggests that there is at least a new consensus about what is wrong, and goes on to suggest what might be right. But it energetically disclaims any connection between this and the views of the rest of the Inspectorate, let alone the DES – and any intention to 'diminish the essential freedom of schools to choose how to carry out their curricular responsibilities . . .' So the conflict between the control and assistance functions is now overt, after the years of suppression – the fact that HMI are prepared to 'take a view' is sufficient to bring the conflict into the open: but it is unresolved. Officially, there is no change: schools can still do exactly what they fancy. Inspectors will influence, cajole, persuade: but not control. And there is no central policy. Whether this new state of affairs will be sufficient to establish a new consensus of action is a matter we shall consider in the next chapter.

So much for HMI, at the start of the third phase of development. Let us see what can be expected of the advisory service, at a time when the emphasis will be on changes in the curriculum system of schools rather than on tinkering with separate subjects. In what ways can advisers further school-based development? We can start by distinguishing between help they might render inside the school, and from outside it. For we have stressed that while the active centre of the change process is the school itself, it will derive ideas and techniques from outside it like any living organism.

The study by Bolam, Smith and Canter makes it plain that there are three reasons why advisers cannot do much to assist the management of change inside the school. First, their role is defined in external terms: their office is in county hall, and they have no teaching commitment or assigned responsibility to an individual school. Second, they face both ways, and so schools cannot be sure how to take their advice once it deals with the whole curriculum and organisation, rather than the desirability of another tape recorder in the French room. And third, they simply haven't the time: we have noted that school visits are short and spasmodic, and an inquiry in the Manchester education department (reported in *The Times Educational Supplement*, 2.12.77) showed that in one week chosen at random, only 25 per cent of advisers' time was spent inside colleges and schools. It must come as no surprise to learn that 63 per cent of the week was spent attending committees, working parties, other meetings or on routine paper work. And we have assumed that advisers have the inclination for school-centred work: the study actually shows that this is the least preferred innovation strategy, and it is also plain that advisers are not trained to do it.

We must quickly remark at this point that in no way are advisers to be reproached for this state of things. For there is, nationally, only one adviser to every 27 schools; rather should they be congratulated for the visits they are able to make, given the bureaucratic pressures from above and the demand for their services from the schools. But appointing more advisers will only ease this present state: it cannot alter the essential limitations of the role. It will make it possible to do more extensively what is already done, but it can have no new effect on the management of curriculum change from within the school. We must recognise, too, that while subject advisers seem logical for a subject-based curriculum, a broad curriculum based on a selection from the culture will involve collaboration between subject specialists and the development of interrelated areas. Subject advisers tend to take the same territorial view of their subject as subject teachers, in the absence of some field of force which can present a unified view which enables them to transcend these established frontiers. This calls for major changes in the way LEAs organise advisory teams: the evidence is that present organisation is rudimentary in the extreme. It does not necessarily follow that subject advisers should no longer be appointed, but rather that advisory policy must be carefully matched to the evolving needs of school-based development.

Consider, for example, the place in the curriculum of an established subject like religious education. If only because of its statutory aspect, most authorities will have an adviser who makes this subject his special interest. And there is much to support the view that religious experience is a distinct form of understanding: all pupils should be brought to see what sorts of ideas and concepts relate to it. But it does not follow that it should exist on the curriculum in a separate block of the timetable. The experience of most schools with single compulsory RE periods is far from happy: the RE teacher, simply in order to survive, often ends up talking about a range of topics, from codes of moral behaviour to environmental pollution. The RE adviser may well see his job as to make sure that genuine RE is taught in these periods.

But this is to miss the point. Although the separate RE periods give the subject an appearance of status, they prevent its being taught in a close relationship with other subjects so as to bring about an advantageous exchange of ideas, and a mutual illumination of these ideas to the benefit of both pupils and teachers. A school might therefore link RE with history and English, and perhaps with geography or social studies, in an interrelated humanities programme. The organisation of the advisory team should reflect and encourage this kind of development, so that the role of the adviser mirrors that of the teachers he advises: he will seek to ensure that the distinctive concepts of religious education survive not by drawing a *cordon sanitaire* around the subject, but by planting it – to change the metaphor – in the richer soil it needs if it is to flourish. Thus the RE adviser might be a member of a humanities team, and the team concept could be given real meaning if it functioned as a team when it went into schools.

Much the same points apply to art and craft advisers: there is everything to be gained from closer links. I have the impression that schools are rather ahead of the advisers in these developments, and it ought to be the other way round. The introduction of new subjects, like social and political education, into the curriculum gives some urgency to the need for redefining advisory policy along more enterprising lines.

In-service courses and school-based change

We must conclude that at least in the medium term, while the future shape of LEA advisory services becomes clearer, the main value of advisers will be in assessing and training. And by seconding themselves, for example, to innovating schools, advisers could acquire first-hand knowledge of what is required in team-based teaching and culture-based curriculum planning. They would then be equipped to devise facilities that could extend professionalism in appropriate directions, and also to help inadequate teachers.

We have noted that arranging courses is an important activity for advisory staff at present, and has largely taken the form of short courses — rarely more than a week in length — in residential centres. Teachers' centres are convenient as a locale for non-residential or part-time courses, and in this third phase of school-based development, a logical extension is to run courses in the school itself. The initiative here usually comes from the head, but it is a development with increasing relevance to the advisory service. Its scope, though, is limited to day conferences, and to initiating rather than installing the innovation. In system-based development, the training role of advisers will be to facilitate, encourage and support.

There will continue to be a place for wholly external courses, but they can amount to only part of the provision. They can assist in curriculum development, but not in managing change in the school. A false start to INSET needs was given by the James Report, which advocated the cyclic release of teachers and so reinforced an externalised view of curriculum change — as the transmission of solutions rather than the study of problems. This was perhaps inevitable, since it was concerned with teachers — probationary teachers, in fact, rather than the curriculum. And at a time when new teachers were still entering the profession in large numbers, its recommendation for a school-based teacher-tutor had some appeal. The further suggestion that the role could be extended to a responsibility for staff development made the job look more important, but was administratively neat rather than educationally logical. And besides, it is another Janus role: how far does the teacher-tutor offer counsel, and how far does he specify what ought to happen? In a few schools, one might find someone with the right psychological qualities to make a go of it: but in most it would appear to be best done by the deputy head, who to some extent has always looked after the needs of staff, and kept an eye on students and probationers.

In any case, even with the limited view taken by the James Report of in-service needs, there is no evidence to support its faith in a course-based model of INSET. Henderson (1978) writes:

> Curiously, for what has become a very expensive industry, very little has been done to see whether the course-based model is living up to the expectations we had of it. . . . Most of the evaluations which have been conducted have confirmed what some perceptive teachers, teacher-trainers, and other educators began to realise in the late 1960s – the course-based model could do some things well, but in many areas it failed dismally to influence practice in our schools.

In the early 1970s a reaction set in against this view of INSET as external to the school, and the term *school-based* took on a special meaning: it implied that in contrast to the course-based model, a school-based model would view the school as a learning community, identifying and resolving its own in-service problems in a self-sufficient fashion. This, of course, has its own dangers: parochialism is the obvious one, and another, as Henderson remarks, is that 'the professional development of the school . . . may dominate the professional development of individual members of its staff, since the needs of the two are not necessarily congruent.'

This is a narrow meaning of the term 'school-based', and it is not one that has been used in this book. Neither, for that matter, has it been implied by the various writers on curriculum (as opposed to INSET) who have talked of the virtues of school-based curriculum development as a way in which the school can become a focus for these activities. As Rudduck (1978) has put it:

A school-based curriculum development of quality cannot emerge from a school that regards itself as self-sufficient. Ideas from the outside are essential. Ideas conveyed through a development project offer a school an opportunity to test the ideas through experience. In this way the ideas of a project come to serve rather than to overwhelm the teacher.

There is, in short, much that external agencies can do to sustain school-based change; and school-based development does not imply an insular, self-contained innovating school. But to avoid any confusion with the narrow meaning of school-based models of INSET, writers on INSET have favoured the term *school-focused* development to describe a model where a synthesis takes place of the course-based and school-based models.

I suggest that we can, for most purposes, regard the terms school-based and school-focused as synonymous. But where the context is one of defining and meeting in-service training and education needs, it is as well to note that a distinction may be intended. What matters here is the needs of schools that have embarked upon system-based change, and what chiefly consigns the James Report to a pigeon-hole is less its failure to get the recipe right in 1972 than its irrelevance to these current circumstances. For not only are there many fewer entrants to the profession; it is also the case that system-based development implies staff collaboration, and in a competently led curriculum team, new and existing staff find an ideal learning environment. Waterhouse (1977a) who, as director of the Avon Resources for Learning Development Unit has offered a service to innovating schools, has noted this:

Staff development is not taking courses . . . [it] is a responsibility and an activity which must be thoroughly integrated with the work of the school. . . . The most effective tutor for staff development is the individual's

immediate superior [who] has all the advantages. . . .
These are advantages which far outweigh the specialist
'personnel' skills of the professional tutor. The only
problem is time. . . .

We are led back again to the school itself, but not any old
school: it must be a school which sees the development of
a broad curriculum as its central activity. If we can get
this right, many INSET aspects are taken care of. But not
all: we are left still with the need to help the school manage
these innovations. And we can see that little help in this
can come from HMI, or advisers, or teachers' centres.

Linkage agencies

We have looked in some detail at the external agents with
whom teachers are most likely to have dealings, and before
we enlarge our inquiries it will help to generalise a little.
In Havelock's terminology (1971), the school is the user
system, and inspectors, advisers and teachers' centres are
elements of resource systems. But linking the two systems
is not a straightforward matter:

Anybody who wants to be effective as a resource person,
as a helper, or as a linker to resources has to know when,
where and how he fits in. Therefore he needs to have
information from the user, not just about what the user
needs but also about how the user goes about solving
problems. . . . The outside resource person must be able
to recapitulate or simulate that internal process.

Havelock associates school-based problem-solving with
linkage agencies, which connect users and client systems
with expert resources and knowledge. The concept is on
all fours with that of the *change agent*, which, in a broad
sense, can refer to any external agent who influences change
in the school. A narrower meaning has been given to the
term as a result of American experience in using external
agents to facilitate change in industry and commerce. Hoyle
(1971) offers a behavioural scientist's model of such an
agent. His relationship with the school is voluntary — he

comes by invitation of head and staff; it is collaborative — he helps to ask questions, rather than imposing answers; power is equalised — head, teachers and change agent can influence each other; he is detached — by virtue of his access to valid knowledge outside the school; and his recommended methods will not be power-coercive, but rely on rational and re-educative strategies. And in another useful typology, Havelock (1969) has distinguished between nine roles for the change or linkage agent: conveyor, consultant, trainer, leader, innovator, defender, knowledge builder, practitioner and user.

We must avoid a doctrinaire approach to the tasks and characteristics of linkage agencies. The value of categories is not to define pure types, but to help us see links between user and resource systems in a fresh light. We are talking about the link between national project and user school, between local policies and school-based change — and, indeed, between theory and practice. Nisbet (1974) has put it in more general terms:

> We train people for educational research, and we train people for teaching, but between the two there is a 'middleman' role which has been seriously neglected. . . . At present there is a group of research workers at one extreme, the body of teachers at the other end, and very few people, stretched beyond their capacities and insufficiently supported by resources, in between. . . . The weak link at present is in the middle, where a support system will need to be developed . . . .

Whether we see the locus of curriculum change inside or outside the school, it is clear that new kinds of intermediate agency are needed. Hoyle (1973) has written that 'The basic premise is that there is a need for roles and institutions intermediate between the school and agencies of curriculum change', and has RDD projects much in mind. He suggests, following James, that *professional centres* might be based in a teachers' centre, college of education, university or polytechnic, and would have four functions: linkage, support, consultancy and in-service training. Linkage would make contacts, resources and information available; support would sustain projects 'after the withdrawal of the development team', and the consultant would provide 'theory, analysis, research and . . . support.' For INSET, the centre would form a 'temporary system' for 'reading, seminars, workshops, visits, assessments of research, and group work'.

The consultancy point is made perhaps more forcibly by Dean (1975), herself a local authority adviser:

> There is a need for a consultancy service, for someone to turn to, whose experience is wider, who can be seen as a peer to be talked with on level terms. This, again, ought to be provided by the employer.

And it has been expanded by Stephens, also an LEA adviser (1975):

> One overwhelming contribution . . . is to extend and to provide for the consultancy based approach to the in-service education of all teachers . . . local authority staff seldom have enough time for deep inquiry, observation, diagnosis and follow-up work. HMI also have, on paper, a consultancy function but in practice do not even offer as much long-term commitment as local-authority staff . . . .

It has been argued here that the agencies of curriculum change are not outside, but inside the schools. We can certainly envisage national projects in key curriculum areas – integrated science is an obvious example – where it would be fatuous for a school, or even a group of schools, to attempt the task of devising new strategies and materials on its own initiative. But here, the existence of professional centres would make it vastly easier to involve schools from the start, and sustain their involvement. And it still holds true that unless the school seeks to make changes of this kind, they will not happen, however lavish the project or numerous the centres – or however explicit national policy might be.

So we must be careful not to institutionalise the concept of the professional centre so that it becomes alienated from its associated schools. Porter, a member of the James committee, has argued (1975) that it would be unsatisfactory for colleges of education and other teacher training bodies to carry out initial training, unless they also have some responsibility for the continuing education of teachers:

> How else will they be able to assess the value of their training . . . and have a base for continuous review and reappraisal . . . of training courses?. . . . The base [of a professional centre] is assumed to be a college of education.

The fallacy here is to assume that the link between initial and continuous training is the college of education, when it is − or ought to be − the school. Few teachers are likely to be enthusiastic about the teacher training college as a curriculum development centre, even though it is certainly a tempting way of occupying redundant college staff. The point about the continuity of training is entirely valid, but would be met by exchange secondments between schools and colleges − in many ways a desirable development in any circumstances.

There are dangers, too, that the teachers' centre as a professional base will succumb to what has been termed an 'oasis' metaphor: a nice place to retreat to, but somehow removed from real life. In any event, there is evidence that secondary teachers rarely visit teachers' centres, and they have been described as mere 'pillar boxes through which curriculum encyclicals are posted' (Thornbury, 1973). For all these reasons, the emphasis placed by Dean and Stephens on school-based consultancy is a confirmation that the people needed in linkage/change-agent roles matter more than an institutionalised centre, and are based in the school rather than outside it. This has implications, too, for course provision which might become a major activity of a professional centre − certainly if based in a reformed college of education − but which may well be an over-rated device for teacher development. Courses need to be geared pretty tightly to the real problems of innovating schools, and the same is true of the professional centre concept. The staff college for schools suggested in the previous chapter is an example of a professional centre which would sustain a close mesh with schools partly by the exchange of staff between schools and college on a secondment basis, and partly by establishing consultancy teams which would be available to schools in its locality. What we should seek to avoid is a centre which appears to exist for its own sake rather than for user schools, and the provision of courses around vague themes using a job lot of speakers and inadequate materials. While many of the courses mounted by LEA advisers are well-conceived, some are certainly pot-boilers — which, considering the work-loads of many advisers, is hardly surprising. One result is that teachers will often say that the real value of courses is the chance to meet other teachers, and that the bar is more useful than the lecture room. A good course must do better than this — and that means discussing real problems, not pseudo-problems.

The staff college concept helps us to get the idea of a professional centre a little clearer. Although its staff would be paid from public funds, its consultancy teams would be seen by the school as independent agents, and thus meet the suggested criteria of a detached, collaborative, non-directive and power-equalised relationship. Stephens (1975) has argued that independence is an important aspect of consultancy:

> It would be a pity if the *only* organised in-service op-
> portunities were in the hands of the employers or if
> *all* the consultants were answerable to the same authority,
> for I readily acknowledge the need to be able to discuss
> problems freely with people who are known to be un-
> connected with the hierarchy at work.

There is an analogy here not only with the independent consultancy services widely used in industry, but also with the use of independent services by local authorities and councils in a variety of fields. Thus a district council would hire a consultant specialising in leisure services to assess not only the demand for, say, a civic hall, but also the ability of the authority to fund it and operate it. And local authority architects' departments have a long-standing tradition of using outside professionals either to ease their own work-load, or to make an independent assessment on a project. No new precedent, therefore, is involved in the suggestion that local education authorities should use their funds to employ consultants specialising in the process of curriculum innovation. The chief obstacle appears to be a failure to recognise the limitations of the advisory service; and this is why the observations of Dean and Stephens, as senior LEA advisers, are of particular interest. They confirm the conclusions of the Bolam, Smith and Canter study, the theoretical work of Havelock, Hoyle and others, and the central thesis of this book.

The Schools Council

In some ways it is remarkable that our discussion of change agencies available to the school has proceeded this far without mentioning the Schools Council. It is, after all, a national body which represents teachers, local authorities and the Department of Education and Science, as well as the universities, examination boards, further education and other interests connected with curriculum and examinations in England and Wales. It has published a string of papers and reports, and sponsored an array of projects which have in turn published teaching materials and documents of various kinds. Its field officers have the degree of independence we have identified as helpful, and as seconded teachers or lecturers should command acceptability. One might assume that, in some way or other, the influence of the council would be felt in every staff room, and have a profounder effect on curriculum planning than HMI or LEA advisers.

The 1978 revision of the council's constitution is a tacit admission that this is not the case, and stems from mounting criticism of its function which was perhaps most firmly put in the DES *Yellow Book* of 1976 with its charges of mediocrity, but which has a broader basis in the trend away from piecemeal planning discussed in the first chapter. The council's allegiance has been to centre-periphery strategies, with the insistent proviso that the prescriptions of the centre are merely options for the periphery. This policy has ensured the worst of both worlds. The national projects, whatever their merits, have had no stable market — and suffer from the well-known disadvantages of RDD strategies. And schools have been encouraged to think that arbitrary choice is a satisfactory form of curriculum planning.

Dissemination is a well-sounding word but an unsatisfactory answer, since it cannot conceal the fact that schools have had no real part in developing projects. And while published documents are certainly necessary, they are not a sufficient way of changing attitudes. The council's real failure is a lack of engagement with the schools: a remarkable irony in view of the substantial teacher representation on its committees. It has a bureaucratic view of teacher involvement, which has parallels with the collectivist systems that can often be spawned in the name of democracy. Consider, for example, the avalanche of paper that has descended on schools in connection with the proposals to replace the GCE A-level examination. No one with the least knowledge of how schools work could suppose that this is the best way of finding out what schools think.

It is almost as if the council is frightened of real grass roots involvement: as if what matters is not what teachers in schools think, but rather what the representatives of their organisations on the Schools Council think. There has certainly been a great reluctance to foster local initiatives, and the same diffidence is evident in the field officer system, which is little more than a token acknowledgment of the need to establish two-way communication with schools. The officers are too few and far between, and have no sooner learnt the ropes than their secondment comes to an end. A further difficulty has been the cumbersome machinery of committees, often leading to the repeated submission of project proposals to bodies whose members have had little time adequately to study their full implications.

The new constitutional arrangements go some way to recognising these criticisms. The review document speaks of the need for 'a speedier, less cumbersome, appraisal and decision-making structure', and a permanent secretary will replace the present system of three seconded joint secretaries. The intention is that much of the council's work should be carried out 'through quite small ad hoc working groups', and the adoption of a two-tier structure means a wider representation of diverse interests on the upper body, the convocation, and effectively loosens the grip of teachers' organisations on the decision-making procedure.

How far these plans succeed in practice will depend on

the skill of the council's staff in making some complex decisions. Its internal politics are far from tranquil, but must be manipulated so as to shape not a limp consensus but a powerful synthesis. More specific matters are the contentious N and F proposals, and the likely implementation of the common system of examination at 16-plus. But the two fundamental issues really stem from the events of the last few years, leading to system-based rather than subject-based development and the view that the curriculum should reflect a wider view of society in its planning, and of the culture in its engagement with pupils. First, there is the matter of the shape of a broader curriculum, and the part the council might play in formulating it. This will be brought into sharp focus when the DES review of LEA curriculum arrangements is published. Second, there is the need to move from centre-periphery to periphery-centre strategies, which raises key questions about the nature of the council's role as a curriculum development agency and the nature of its field structure. And behind both issues is the question of control: the Inspectorate has moved into this arena, and the Taylor report has given teachers' organisations a convenient opportunity to stress the virtues of professional autonomy. And in any local initiatives, the co-operation of the LEAs will be crucial. At present, one of the most hopeful aspects of the council's review arrangements is perhaps their favourable reception by the LEAs. But to forge wide-ranging and self-consistent policies that can assure the council a leading part in the educational changes of the next five years will call for a sure touch: not least because, to achieve an impact, the council must be seen by the schools as a more credible force for change than in the past.

The Schools Council's present dilemma has been summed up by Owen (1977), a former joint secretary:

> The council is trapped. It cannot extend its activities in the development of curriculum without rejustifying itself in terms of the Green Paper. It cannot argue for an extension of development which is simply innovative . . . . In attempting to create a broad spread of influence, separate from the effects of single projects, the council

has depended upon the appeal of its publications and upon the work of its field officers. The latter are too few, too temporary and too loosely committed, as it seems, to the broad aims of the council to have had much chance of lasting success. Publications about educational development have multiplied too rapidly to allow the council to maintain its particular distinction.

National projects and school-based development

Some suggestions about the council's future role will be made in the next chapter. For the moment we are focusing on what we can extrapolate from its past performance, and one of the later projects – the Geography 14–18 Project – explicitly faces the criticisms that have left scars on earlier projects, and indicates how national projects might usefully contribute to a pattern of school-based development. It is described in some detail in the Open University case study *Portrait of a National Project* (1976) by J. Reynolds, its last director:

> National projects alone are in a position both to analyse curriculum needs in relation to cultural trends *and* initiate major programmes of cultural intervention. . . . Curriculum thought and action are attempts to find accommodations between ideals of good classroom learning and the perceptions of other people which condition what is practicable.

The project's approach recognises three elements in an 'enabling framework for curriculum renewal':

i   The involvement of teachers in the varied processes of curriculum design;

ii The production of a variety of curriculum guidelines and materials which exemplify not only new content in geography but learning strategies and means of evaluation;

iii A supporting examination system that reduces some of the inflexibility of present systems and fosters the project's curriculum priorities.

145

The project has therefore, from the beginning, involved its associated schools and their LEAs with its intentions. It is interesting to note that, in discussing the use of LEA advisers as 'gatekeepers' to allow projects to enter schools, Bolam, Smith and Canter (1976) comment: 'The Geography 14–18 Project's strategy of obtaining the support of an inspector and appointing a consortium coordinator was likely to be effective and successful.' But we must also note that these admirable intentions, and the theory of curriculum change which supports them, had a bumpy passage through the Schools Council committees. For example, the rationale of the project was prepared for the council in 1970, and declared:

> The questions are 'How can we keep school geography up to date in the light of changes both within the subject and within society at large?' To answer the question, it helps to think of the total curriculum system. No simple formulation . . . in terms of immediate classroom needs is likely to take into account adequately the interdependence of social relations, institutions, organisational patterns and values which lie at the core. . . . The question . . . is rather 'Why does the necessity for curriculum projects arise?'

This is a very good question, and it would have helped if the Schools Council had brooded upon it since its very inception. But the Report of the council's steering committee B (16.11.72) gives this kind of approach short shrift:

> There was criticism that the project's purpose had been deflected by theoretical digressions. In reply, Mr J. B. Reynolds, research fellow with the project, insisted that there must be a sound theoretical base for good curriculum development.

And a week later, steering committee C reported that 'while a lot of work and thought had been put into its production, much of [a proposed working paper's] content was more appropriate to learned journals than a working paper.' We can see here the practical man's suspicion of theory beginning, perhaps, to border on the philistine. As it turns out, the project seems to be popular with schools and is likely to prove one of the council's more successful ventures.

Research approaches and teacher practice

So the birth-pangs of this project highlight not only some effective strategies for national and local intervention; they expose the conflict between theory and practice at the primary planning level. There are genuine difficulties here which can have the most important consequences for the role of external agencies in curriculum change, and we shall conclude this chapter by looking at them more closely. At school level, we have already remarked on the convoluted language in which research utterances are often cloaked, even when the research is applied — in the sense of looking at real classroom problems — rather than pure. The consequence is a reluctance by teachers to identify with a research paradigm, and this can drive teacher and researcher still further apart. One reason for this seeming remoteness between theoretical work and practical problems is that most theory is construed within one or other of the established contributory disciplines: philosophy, psychology, sociology and history. Then the problems within a field of application like curriculum studies are seen within the conceptual structure of a particular discipline. Skilbeck (1976b) has argued that a problem-centred approach, which tries to bring insights from a variety of disciplines to bear on questions arising from the experience of teachers, may be more fruitful, because:

i   Aspects of the disciplines are necessary for an understanding of curriculum, but not sufficient;
ii A problem- and theme-based approach is an economical and effective way of drawing together knowledge and understanding yielded by the great variety of subjects which have a bearing on curriculum decisions;
iii The bulk of curriculum literature . . . does not take the form of applied disciplines, but has its own language and thought structure.

A further reason has more to do with the practice of teaching than the methods and language of theory. It is surprising that the most helpful study of classroom practice was carried out ten years ago, and on American elementary school teachers (Jackson, 1968). But there is no doubt its conclusions ring true in the setting of English secondary schools, on the whole. A useful discussion of Jackson's work is given in Hoyle (1972). It appears that four themes are of importance in the way teachers judged their work and gained satisfaction from it. First, *Immediacy*: they emphasised the present, and pupils' spontaneous responses, even though the school focuses on long-term aims; second, *Informality*: they emphasised their informal relations with pupils, while retaining responsibility and authority; three, *Autonomy*: while they welcomed guidelines and collaboration, they felt 'most comfortable with the classroom door closed and the curriculum guides tucked away in the supplies closet' (Jackson, 1968). Finally, *Individuality*: they assessed their success as teachers from their personal observations of their pupils. They knew when they were succeeding from the look on their faces.

There is perhaps nothing very surprising about all this. Jackson's teachers had been identified as successful by their superiors, and these sound like teachers who deserve to succeed, because they are responding all the time to the way their pupils perceive and appreciate the ideas and concepts they seek to impart. But we must note what they did not do: they did not have behaviourally-precise objectives, nor were they sympathetic to objective evaluation. As Davies (1976) has put it:

> Jackson . . . found that classroom expertise coexisted with an inability to rationalise the very categories of child-centred discourse. His sample taught through the seats of their skirts.

It seems likely that most teachers do not look for complicated causes, are intuitive rather than rational, and are reluctant to abandon present practices. It follows that the actual business of teaching is equally at odds both with the methods of research and the planning of curriculum on a broader scale. But this does not mean that teachers cannot, in the nature of things, lift their horizons from the immediacies of the classroom and adopt a different perspective, a different style of reasoning. After all, Jackson's analysis might suggest that teachers would have difficulty in reconciling themselves to the formal techniques of external examinations, but there is no evidence that in practice this is such a tremendous wrench. We can conclude that just as examination technique is seen as an acquired art for pupil and teacher, so also must be those techniques which teachers need in working with others to plan the curriculum and devise materials and teaching strategies. We cannot, in short, assume that good teachers come equipped with these skills: on the contrary, they call to some extent for modes of analysis and appraisal which conflict with the necessarily intuitive wisdom of the classroom.

We can perhaps draw a parallel with the organised structures of knowledge which a doctor can call upon in reflecting upon a particular case – and which a medical school will call upon in devising its courses – and the personal response he must make in the consulting room, which will owe as much to his perceptions of the patient as an individual as to the knowledge he needs to diagnose and prescribe. But the intuitive response of the surgery does not determine his whole strategy of professional judgment: his concept of professionalism must be broad enough to recognise that circumstances alter cases, and decisions can imply different valuative structures. In the same way, teachers cannot afford to dismiss theory because it is unfamiliar, or too abstract, or simply unlike life in classrooms: they must learn how to judge it on its own terms, so as to decide on its weaknesses and strengths, and use it to help them plan the curriculum.

While, therefore, we can understand the instinctive reactions of the Schools Council's steering committees B and C, we cannot accept them. And, of course, this broader basis of judgment is necessary not only for teachers, but for those outside the schools who are likely to be increasingly involved in curricular decisions, and who may find the language of curriculum studies uphill work. And if we may take our medical analogy a stage further, we can see another complicating factor. For the purpose of medicine is clear enough, as is that of schools: doctors promote health, and schools promote education. But while health is a concept carrying such universal acceptance that its meaning is effectively unchanged in all industrial countries, the concept of education means one thing to an industrialist, another to a head teacher, still another to a parent. So the business of educational innovation is peculiarly fraught with uncertainties and irrelevancies, and calls for decision-making procedures which must reconcile to an unusual extent lay opinion and an enlarged professionalism.

We can conclude on an optimistic note, for evidence exists that teachers can acquire these further professional skills. It comes from Shipman's study (1974) of the Schools Council Keele Integrated Studies Project, and in particular of the work of the seconded teachers who acted as co-ordinators between the project team and the user schools. They quickly assumed the role of curriculum developers and change agents:

> These teachers not only picked up the skills in establishing social relations within a large number of schools, not only became practised at addressing meetings and guiding other teachers, not only got used to writing curriculum materials for publication, but rapidly picked up insights into the problems that they faced. . . . This ability to see the source and context of problems was in striking contrast to the teachers in the schools. . . . Yet this had been done quickly and without any training programme. It was the local horizons and narrow terms of reference of the teachers that formed the main barrier to genuine implementation.

Teachers, like pupils, rise to the expectations that the school has of them. Once a school can be thrown into a higher state of excitation, so that the familiar and humdrum is transformed by a wider vision and a new purpose, then teachers extend themselves to meet these new responsibilities. In this case, the project was concerned solely with the humanities area of the curriculum, and a particular difficulty was the lack in the schools of any rationale of the whole curriculum which would help the teachers to see its wider implications. The energising force had to come from the project alone. And the co-ordinators were learning by doing, and had to do so within the context of the project as the innovating agency. The value of developmental activity as a form of in-service education comes over very clearly:

> The clue to successful innovation may lie not so much in in-service training, but in the secondment of teachers to research and development teams.

The great strength of school-based development is that the teams are to be found in the school itself, and once again the logic of in-service initiatives which relate intimately to the needs of the innovating school is very evident. The professional centre must be sufficiently staffed and funded to act as an initiating agency, but supple enough to provide an individualised service as the innovation takes place over time. A subtle balance needs to be struck between the detachment that will make it a unit for fresh thinking in its own right, and the remoteness of a training institution running courses which are out of touch with school realities.

The vital element has to be that of the consultancy team, which does for the whole-curriculum review process what the co-ordinators did in the Keele project. And the Keele experience suggests that the chain reaction will continue; the school becomes a breeder reactor, and the external change agents are free to accept an invitation from another institution. This deals with the criticism, frequently made by developers with a centre-periphery turn of mind, that the cost of a consultancy service would limit its application to a handful of schools, and facilities would be inadequate to meet the demand for in-service training once it had been generated. The truth is that a little of the right sort of help goes a very long way: simply because there is no substitute for the challenging experience which gives the teacher a firm framework for action, but obliges him to find in himself new perceptions and new talents. That experience can be worth any number of INSET courses, and can turn a teacher into a developer and a change agent in his own right.

Chapter 6

Strategies for Regeneration

If we are to regenerate the curriculum, we must have an understanding of how it functions at present, a new goal to aim for, and confidence in our ability to reach it. Of these, the new goal is perhaps the most elusive. For the longer we look at the process of education, the more we see of its complexity. At one extreme, we might react by limiting our vision to piecemeal improvement; at the other, by postulating a utopian solution which chooses to transcend reality rather than come to terms with it.

Neither of these will do. Innovation on the instalment plan certainly narrows the target, but it also narrows our perception of the interactive nature of curriculum change. The part is stressed at the expense of the whole, and because the change process has not cut deep enough, the innovation is unlikely to last. Our vision must be broad enough to take in all the curriculum architecture, but breadth need not imply impractical dreams. Now that a normative climate for whole-curriculum change is beginning to take shape, system-based development can be unified as cultural synthesis and take practical account of the school's organic unity.

We have examined these aspects of regeneration from the differing perspectives of school, head, teacher, pupil and external agent, and our task is now to suggest strategies and initiatives in the domain of choice and action. We have seen, too, that there are different ways of looking at the change process, and our inclination must be to view schools as organisms rather than mechanisms. Analytical approaches are valuable, but it is the humanity of a school which will overcome constraints and make new ideas work. Owen (1973) has drawn attention to this:

> If education improves, develops, changes or differs in any way from decade to decade, it is because particular people in particular fields have had the patience, good fortune, insight and good experience which is necessary to make them credible when they wish to commend something to other people.

Credibility is an attribute of people rather than ideas or organisations, and it is the credibility of change agents which makes a continuous process out of change-events.

It is the fact that education is a living, political concept implemented by people for the benefit of others that restricts parallels with comparable systems. Miles (1964), for example, has noted that the rate of introducing new ideas in educational systems lags behind those in medical, industrial and agricultural systems, and suggests three reasons:

i   There is an absence in education of any body of valid scientific research findings;

ii There is a lack of change agents in order to promote new educational ideas;

iii Very little economic incentive exists to adopt even those ideas and innovations which have been explored, and which on the face of it appear to have some logical validity.

Let us look briefly at these in turn. The first acknowledges the problematic nature of educational questions; we cannot assert optimum learning conditions in the way we can the optimum reaction conditions for a chemical process. The same reservation must hold for attempts to evaluate educational outcomes. But we can find out enough to shift the balance of probabilities, even if it merely forces us to reconsider our original assumptions. The work by Burstall *et al.* (1974), for example, on French in primary schools suggests, if nothing else, that assumptions about the optimum age to start learning French need to be questioned. We cannot be certain: but we can eliminate some of the improbabilities from our hunches if we choose to.

Miles's second point about the need for change agents is still true, but there are signs that we have now learnt enough about curriculum development projects to recognise the importance of them in problem-solving strategies in particular. The third point, about economic incentives in education, reflects partly the failure of educational processes to yield to cost-effective criteria, and also the reluctance of society to accord the same concept of built-in obsolescence to education and schooling as it does to the manufacture of other consumer goods. While parents will readily accept that a kind of contemporary efficiency should govern their choice of motor car, sentiment and nostalgia prevail if they are choosing a school. The influence of childhood memories is part of the story: even parents who hated their traditional grammar school would not want their children to miss the experience. But there is also perhaps the feeling that the case for innovation is unproven. It is an instinctive feeling, but it is there; and it has often been justified.

We must show that our professional understanding of what school should be about is as convincing and self-consistent as a parent's tranquilly-conceived recollection of it. Hence the importance of a rationale of the whole curriculum which presents the completeness of education, and does so in terms which parents can not only appreciate, but themselves enlarge on and contribute to. For progress is, as Isaiah Berlin has remarked, a kind of parricide: the attitudes of people are central to innovation, and we must put our faith not merely in courses and resources, but in the ability of people to change the attitudes of other people.

We shall examine strategies of regeneration by considering the particular before the general. After examining the ways in which the change process might begin in schools, we shall look at a recent national strategy for whole-curriculum change, and then consider a variety of possible approaches at national, regional and local levels.

Initiating innovation in schools

The change process in schools will follow one of three prior states: it may be a *new school*; or an existing school may undergo an *external impetus*; or it may respond to an *internal* impetus.

The *new school* is at first sight particularly propitious. Head and staff can view the curriculum as a *tabula rasa*; there are no existing arrangements to cramp their style, and no existing staff to convert or placate. And if the school is able to grow year by year, this will be a further advantage. In practice not all these circumstances will prevail, but the odds are favourable enough to make the new school a clear case in itself. Yet it seems likely that the opportunity thus offered is rarely seized. I have written (Holt, 1978) of the new approaches to the comprehensive school curriculum that we were able to develop at Sheredes School in Hertford-shire from its inception in 1969. In the ensuing years the progress of reorganisation made me aware of a number of other new-school openings, and I recall discussing with a lecturer in education the possibility of DES funding for a conference of heads with these experiences in common. Unfortunately this came to nothing. But I was struck by the conventionality of the curriculum arrangements which most of these developing schools preferred to adopt. I have already mentioned some notable exceptions: Countesthorpe, Stantonbury and Sidney Stringer come to mind. And there are certainly others. But the point to note is that favourable circumstances — what I have termed change-events — are of no avail without change-agents. Undoubtedly the key agent must be the head: if only because he will be the first member of the staff to be appointed. And because he can sub-sequently appoint staff who are receptive — as far as he and they can determine — to the new curriculum, then the school is able to benefit from a steady supply of new change-agents in the shape of successive new and existing teachers. In summary, there are two reasons why the new school might be a fruitful innovative proposition: a distinctive set of change-events which need have no localised historical associations, and a continuous supply of change-agents from within the school itself.

This does not mean that the innovating new school can afford to cut itself off from outside sources of advice and stimulus. At Sheredes we recognised the need for linkage agencies early on, and attempted to get a county curriculum development association off the ground in 1970. Its failure was due not to a lack of interest on the part of individual teachers, but a general apathy at that time towards whole-curriculum planning. The prime focus of curriculum activity was seen to be the development of Mode 3 CSE syllabuses in individual subjects. We were subsequently dependent on our analysis of Schools Council project strategies and materials; on individual contacts with university research departments; and on published theoretical studies. And the feeling that a school is making its own way can keep morale high. That the outcome was, in the event, satis-factory was due to the internally-generated perceptions of the staff, the support of parents and governors, and the tradition of school autonomy which is the Hertfordshire inheritance from Newsom's stewardship.

It should be noted that in two respects, the new school will experience constraints. First, the curriculum slate will not have been wiped as clean as first sight suggests. There will be national and local views to take into account: in 1969, for example, some of the Sheredes governors were unenthusiastic about my suggestion that Spanish or German might be a good choice for the first foreign language, and it seemed wiser to adopt French, as the other schools in the neighbourhood had already. And second, the new school is likely to attract staff near the start of their careers. This means it will be long on energy, but short on experience. And however much the school will want to reward its teachers by internal promotion, not all the Indians can become chiefs. Resolving the resulting tensions will depend partly on the buoyancy of the national market. To some extent, though, the mechanism is self-correcting: when jobs are hard to get, maturer teachers will settle for helping to start up a new school, even if they must wait four years for examination work. Parental choice will tighten the first constraint. At Sheredes, for example, for some years there was a surplus of school places in the area, and we were in competition with a reorganised former grammar school only a mile away. Even so, a new school offering a common curriculum within a non-streamed format was able to attract first-choice support and obtain a fully representative spread of ability.

This undoubtedly reflected the sensitivity and good advice that the school's governors were able to provide. And while Becher and Maclure (1978) may fairly remark that

> school-based development also very clearly shows how far the head of a school and his staff — temporary incumbents of a public institution — are able and encouraged to stamp their own values on a school . . .

— it should be added that unless these values are shared by governors and parents, they will be as temporary as the staff and attract indifferent support wherever parental choice is a factor. Head and staff have a professional duty to work out a consistent set of values to underpin the curriculum: but this must take account of community attitudes too. It is a matter of formulating and negotiating values; stamping or imprinting will have no staying power. The role of the governors is crucial, and at Sheredes School the opportunity to co-opt representatives of the staff and of the parents was taken as soon as it was made possible, early in the life of the school, by an initiative of the local authority. And when after eight years the governors came to appoint a new head, their commitment to the continuation of the existing curriculum and organisation was made quite explicit.

The second kind of change will begin with an *external impetus* to an existing school. It can arise as a result of combination with another school, reorganisation into a comprehensive, or the appointment of a new head. The influence of the head is so significant that this must be counted an event of marked change potential. The feature common to change-events of this type is that although the potential is strong, the head — and in some cases staff too — will bear, in the short term, a substantially increased administrative load. The discontinuity in the school's life which releases forces for change, also diverts the head's time and energy at precisely the moment when his attention could profitably be given to the process of initiating whole-curriculum change. This is in contrast to the more gradual way in which the head of a new school takes up increasing responsibilities as the school grows.

It is clear that the headships of several hundred schools must change hands every year: no data on these important events seem to be available. It follows that this is much the most common way in which external change-events arise in the school system, and it would make sense to consider how heads might be helped to make the best of their opportunities. An obvious device would be a pre-appointment induction course at a staff college, while an acting head, if necessary, holds the fort for a term. The head-designate would be in active touch with his new school, but quite free from day-to-day management and as far as possible from policy decisions. He would visit the school to appoint any new staff; to gain first-hand knowledge of the school's ethos, special attributes and defined problems; and to meet his senior staff. His induction course would thus be directly related to his new brief, and the information he derives about the school would form a key input for discussions and exercises, in addition to the theoretical work on curriculum, management and organisation which has been discussed in chapter 4. The new head would also take part in curriculum planning and team teaching exercises in conjunction with the local schools with which the staff college co-operated; visit schools and linkage agencies; and act as a co-opted member of the college's consultancy teams so as to gain a broad perspective of school curriculum, and see the value of independent consultancy in establishing system-based change. His sponsoring LEA would also arrange to give him an introduction to their procedures, and to meet the officers with whom he will have dealings.

The cost of this innovation would almost certainly be recouped from the smoother running of the school as a result of it. It is easy to forget that an error of judgment in a school can be very expensive. A trivial matter such as ordering the wrong type of furniture means many phone calls, visits and substantial administrative expense. The time of LEA officers does not come cheap. A more serious matter like a mishandling of a parent or teacher could involve the intervention of the press, teachers' organisations, governors and lawyers. Making sure that the consequences are not as disturbing as this will mean a flurry of meetings, letters and consultations at a high level.

But the real gain would, of course, be the conversion of the head into a change-agent with an informed perspective on curriculum development and an understanding of techniques of implementation. He will already have been able to obtain independent opinions on possible strategies in his new school, and he will value the provision of similar professional services as he takes up the reins of office. And his connections with the staff college, once established, form a continuing resource which he can use both informally and in attending refresher courses or in supplying case study material. For it is not enough that the new head be left as an unsupported change-agent: he will need to convert existing staff into agents for change in their own right, and to do that he will need help. So will his staff: once the school has framed new curriculum approaches which carry the support of the governors, it should qualify for a special LEA grant of money for resource equipment and materials, the right to the services for a given period of a consultant or consultancy team, and a given amount of in-service education measured, possibly, as a fixed quota of days for which the absence of staff — whether on courses, visits or study sessions — would be covered by supply staff.

Measures of this sort may sound expensive: but the fact is that much LEA expenditure finds its way into curriculum support work, under one heading or another, which may be costly and of doubtful value. It is also likely to be concerned with specific areas of the curriculum, rather than the whole curriculum. For example, a number of LEAs have supported schemes for computer-assisted learning: perhaps in first-year mathematics programmes based on individualised learning. It has now emerged that — far from showing savings on normal teaching methods — the cost of these approaches is a substantial additional amount. The point is that even in times of financial difficulty, money can be found, and is being found, for projects with an 'add-on' cost element. A further advantage of the proposals made here is that at least a proportion of INSET funds — I would suggest a major proportion — is directly associated with whole-curriculum development.

The third kind of change-events will be the result of internal impetus. The impetus thus offered need not necessarily be weaker than in either of the two previous cases, and there will not be the additional administrative burden associated with external impetus. The school will be functioning normally, but suggestions will be made for new curriculum developments either at the initiative of the head, or as a result of new staff, or at the initiative of existing staff. It may well be that news has reached the school of innovations at a nearby school as a result of a new head and the kind of scheme outlined above. The assumption in all cases is that the head is disposed to encourage the interest aroused by the change-events rather than stifle it. This, of course, is where the normative climate for system-based change will be a decisive influence.

The prime need here is for an input to the school that can help the head frame the right questions, and help the school to define the essential curriculum problems. Given a staff college provision, LEAs could offer priority support for heads to attend the college who, with their schools, seemed to have reached this stage of ripeness and readiness. An alternative intervention — always, of course, at the request of head and staff — could come from some established regional resource. A consultancy team from a professional centre would be an attractive strategy. A day conference might be a useful beginning: but it is only a beginning. It calls for a substantial follow-up with the kind of INSET and support-service help already outlined.

However apt and extensive the contingent support, there is no assumption here that schools can change, as it were, overnight. We must recognise that system-based change takes time, and will have its own natural pace. A school might well begin by making a situational analysis of the external and internal factors which define its state: cultural and parental expectations, changing subject-matter; its pupils, teachers and ethos (see, for example, Skilbeck, 1976c). It might then define a short-term goal in terms of immediate, perceived needs — possibly reform of part of the timetable, which might have provoked the change-events in the first place. But a longer-term policy strategy may well also emerge: it will be taken into account in the short-term improvements, but will require more time for study, and more resources. A programme of school-based development can be set up, with a view to initiating the new curriculum at first-year level in, say, eighteen months' time. Some modifications might at first be required because of the demands of the existing curriculum and timetable, but these can be identified and discussed and solutions agreed by appropriate working parties. The eighteen months' lead time will be maintained as staff teams prepare learning strategies and teaching materials for each successive year as the new curriculum moves up the school. The parents of existing pupils will have played their part in the original deliberations, and the parents of the pupils who will embark on the new programme in their first year will have had its intention and execution explained to them in a series of meetings at the school and at feeder primaries. LEA advisory staff will ensure that necessary INSET support is phased in, interpret county decisions to the school which might have a bearing on the innovation, and throughout the authority control the climate so as to make it as favourable as possible to departures of this kind. And school-specific professional services will be made available so as to assist the process in the school of cultural re-definition and synthesis. In this way, some seven years after the original change-events were exploited, the school will end up with a new whole curriculum which, all along, will reflect current thinking and available developments but will put them in a total context rather than a haphazard, unrelated one. By the end of that time, many of the instigating staff will have left: but continuity will be assured by the systematic planning introduced from the first, and backed up by LEA support from advisers and professional centres.

This seems a perfectly feasible scenario for system-based change. But it implies a very different approach from what we have at present. Bolam (1974) has written:

There now exists a whole range of change-agent roles in education: advisers, advisory teachers, teacher-tutors; teachers' centre wardens; college lecturers; curriculum developers; Schools Council field officers. What we lack is any detailed knowledge of the way in which such people actually help teachers in schools and the way in which teachers perceive and value this help.

The indications are that the activities of most of these agents are peripheral to the change process in the school, because the change process — and its needs — have been conceived as external to the school. Eraut (1972) has made a similar point:

> Traditional forms of in-service education seemed to be concerned more with the transmission of solutions than with the study of problems . . . the pattern has been modelled on pre-service education and largely ignores the fact that the participants are often experienced teachers with as much to contribute as to receive . . . all too often teacher centre leaders, lacking guidance on other possible modes of work, have reverted to the tradition of running courses in the usual lecture-discussion mode.

The impression often given to teachers has been: this is how we see it — these are the questions we are asking — now it's up to you to provide the answers. This has a deceptive look of teacher involvement about it: but the point is that INSET must start with the teachers' questions and solutions, rather than those of the trainers and advisers. And there is a need not only to deploy existing agencies in more effective ways, but to create new agencies that are essential to the management of curriculum change within the school. And we must place initiatives of this kind in the context of the national and local scene.

A national initiative

A useful way of approaching this more generalised viewpoint is to consider briefly the strategy for whole-curriculum change that has been presented in the HMI document *Curriculum 11–16* (1978). This must, after all, be seen as a unique attempt to influence the politics of the curriculum, and it makes no bones about its belief that the curriculum must have a broad cultural base:

> pupils are members of a complicated civilization and culture, and it is reasonable to argue that they have nothing less than a right to be introduced to a selection of its essential elements.

Talk about pupils' rights can, of course, be misleading: it is not a straightforward concept to interpret. It is arguable that the notion of compulsory schooling implies in itself that schools must offer a curriculum which gives equality of access to knowledge. Davies (1976), for example, refers to

> the prototypical twentieth-century statement as to the desirability of equality of opportunity . . . on the necessitous basis of common induction.

And Warnock (1977) points out that 'If equality is really what we are after, then . . . it is more conducive to equality for people to study roughly the same things at school than radically different things.' It may seem needlessly rigorous to fuss about the reasons for a new departure when it is plainly setting out for the right destination. But the development of a common curriculum is a complex matter, and those involved in the business will need to go back again and again to the basic principles. However: we can see that the concern of this document is with cultural mapping in some rationally acceptable form, and look next to an account of how it is to be done.

But we are given barely an inkling of how the mandatory 'areas of experience' — aesthetic and creative, ethical, linguistic, mathematical, physical, scientific, social and political, spiritual — are to be explained and justified; of how pupils are to think their way through to these utopian outcomes. There are a number of papers on separate subjects which suggest content in more detail, but no indication of how this content and an appropriate methodology might be derived from a self-consistent set of valuative judgments. There is no discussion of the implications of a common culture curriculum for the professionalism of the teacher which rises above the level of platitude:

> There is a lot to be said for all those concerned with the drawing up and teaching of curricula defining their aims and objectives and trying to think within the context of wider needs, rather than solely with reference to their own circumstances.

The tone here, as elsewhere, is patronising: certainly teachers need to widen their horizons beyond subject-based routines, but is this the right way to suggest it? And in curriculum innovation, the way you do it is just as important as what you are trying to do.

Two further points are worth mentioning. The central importance of interrelated work is never faced. Almost as an afterthought, in a section on timetabling, we read that:

> It must be stressed that the common curriculum is almost certainly interdependent in concept, though this is not a necessary condition for its timetabling. . . . The common curriculum is concerned, in short, with integrated attitudes and a self-consistent conceptual framework: it is not concerned with subjects, whether integrated or not, except as labels of convenience.

This is a narrowing view of the usefulness of subject structures, calling at least for a more extended interpretation than is given here. Teachers without some experience of common-curriculum approaches are unlikely to find this passage very helpful.

A second point of interest arises in a paper on 'staffing structures'. The intention here is to offer models 'which might enable curriculum theory to be put into practice more easily'. But the decision-making process is shown as rather nightmarish block diagrams bearing serpentine arrows, and committees with titles like 'pupil policy', 'staff development', 'finance and resources', 'additions and target levels', and 'bases and content'. The general impression is confusing. One is reminded of Vickers's summary (1973) of the philosophy of those who, in the name of technology, have a preoccupation with non-human processes and non-human ways of thinking: 'Efficiency in operations results from arranging conditions of work in such a way that human elements interfere to a minimum degree.' And communication, Vickers argues,

> is limited not by the means to send messages but by the organisation at the receiving end. . . . The means for interpreting messages are in total confusion. . . . The major threat . . . is the lack of an appreciative system sufficiently widely shared to mediate communication,

sufficiently apt to guide action and sufficiently acceptable to make personal experience bearable . . . a system to describe the inter-connected set of largely tacit standards of judgment by which we both order and value our experience.

Drawing up systems-inspired diagrams of staffing structures shows the same error of prescription as the list of areas of experience for the common curriculum. It is the centre-periphery approach yet again: the external recipe offering solutions, rather than insight and analysis that can show schools how to start with problems. And in any case, structures of the kind presented will do nothing to mediate communication, guide action or make personal experience bearable: they are more likely to confuse and alienate.

The foreword to the document mentions that 'five local authorities are supporting a number of their schools who are working on this framework', and it is interesting to note that this recognises the need for supporting schools which embark on system-based development after an external impetus. And we must presume that this support extends to a consideration of the issues not dealt with in the document which, as it stands, seems insensitive to some matters of critical importance.

Levels of planning and intervention

We shall now take a wider view and see what kind of support structures and initiatives are likely to be advisable if we are to regenerate school curricula, and see the process as school-based. Skilbeck (1975) has suggested local, regional and national levels of provision and control. To teachers' centres at the local level, he would add 'a great deal more of structural in-filling', including

the universal adoption of the principle of substituting for teachers participating in courses and workshops. . . . This in-filling is essentially for the purposes of facilitating exchange of experience . . .

At the regional level, Skilbeck suggests a support structure

165

in urban areas of 100,000 population, and rural areas of rather less:

> It is only at the regional level, if at all, that it will be possible to provide comprehensive resource centres. . . . Funding for regional resource centres will be more demanding than regional resources alone can sustain and should become a national responsibility. . . . A considerable amount of national control and development activity can and should be transferred to regional centres . . . . Such changes would have implications for the Schools Council . . .

Skilbeck considers that national curriculum development activities should be diminished; policy formation, though, 'a decided weakness in British education, is a national function with clear political overtones, and it is essentially this which needs to be strengthened at the national level'.

For Lawton (1977b), a further advantage of curriculum planning at three or four levels is that it makes for sensible power-sharing:

> There is a dangerous tendency to think that there is only one level of curriculum planning and that therefore there must be a struggle for control of the curriculum. Central government has a perfect right to say that compulsory education for every child ought to include offering that child scientific understanding, but it must be left to the school exactly how to achieve scientific understanding.

Lawton argues that at the national level, there is a role for the Schools Council in laying down certain guidelines: 'not a detailed curriculum, but . . . the knowledge and experiences every school should be obliged to offer.' Local education authorities would form the next level, and would advise schools on the interpretation of national guidelines. Schools would have 'the major responsibility: translating national guidelines into detailed curriculum plans . . . a planning exercise involving the majority of the staff.' And at the fourth level, teachers would be free to plan and teach within the agreed curriculum:

> Surely professional autonomy does not mean every teacher

166

having absolute freedom to do whatever he wants, but implies acting in accordance with agreed professional standards?

The three levels of national, regional and local interpretation do, of course, already exist. But their curriculum, control and training functions are not always clear-cut, and result from accident rather than design. Thus GCE O-level and CSE examinations, working within a vague and unwritten consensus of a hierarchy of subjects, are effectively a national level of control: they are the responsibility of the Schools Council, which has also launched a number of national curriculum projects. The DES, after a passive role for some years, has begun to show curriculum activity, and recognises the importance of INSET (which the Schools Council is constitutionally unable to become involved in, although it ties in well with its concern for dissemination). At the regional or LEA level, control exists through advisers, officers and governing bodies in a variable fashion. It is fair to say that on the whole, curriculum issues have, in the past, been of little interest to LEA members or staff. A new education committee chairman may have an enthusiasm, say, for the EEC, and encourage schools to twin with others across the Channel: a CEO may seek to foster religious education. But it is doubtful if most LEA officers — and certainly some advisers — make a point of informing themselves about curriculum studies. Indeed, LEAs are in general not aware of the curricular arrangements in their schools, and no doubt this is one reason why the Secretary of State is asking them to find out and tell her. Their training involvement is through advisers and teachers' centres, and tends to lie in subject areas and dissemination rather than school-based problem-solving.

The clearest responsibility is at school level, since this is where the buck stops. So it is really no surprise that the head is allowed the considerable power necessary to determine policy and resolve conflicts. His opposite number in, say, West Germany is much more circumscribed. The school may not be free, for example, to choose any new English course: the *Land* or regional government will establish a committee of teacher and higher education representatives to draw up an approved textbook list. While the use of a particular course is unlikely to be enforced, the recommendations of the central body will not be without influence.

The British system is more pluralist and potentially more responsive. It offers scope for deep-structure innovation, but little protection against mediocrity. It demands more of heads and teachers, and probably gets it: we expect, for example, teachers to act *in loco parentis* during the day, and attend after-school meetings and functions, and nothing much is written down about this; most teachers react in a human fashion and give in generous measure. Central systems are more susceptible to political influence, but aim to guarantee a sound basic level of performance. There is less room for manoeuvre and local variation, but less likelihood of serious shortfall. The system expects competence rather than enthusiasm, and is prepared to pay for it in tighter structures and clearer conditions.

The last ten years or so of secondary reorganisation and curriculum development have not shown the British system to advantage. This is because decentralised systems respond to the prevailing valuative mood of the times, unless some political initiative imposes a new framework. There was no such initiative, and so novelty and free choice became the twin lodestars of curriculum planning, as of commerce and popular culture. Such school innovation as occurred was mainly subject-based: the few system-based developments were often flawed by a tendency to emphasise the part (for example, individualised learning, integrated studies or participatory democracy) at the expense of the whole.

Now the mood has changed, and politicians of all parties are eager to talk of the need to raise educational standards. The DES Assessment of Performance Unit plans to monitor achievement across the curriculum, and the 1977 DES Green Paper seeks to establish a framework for the curriculum. The Inspectorate has published a document advocating a common curriculum to occupy 'two thirds or more of the total time available', and launched a pilot scheme to implement these proposals. And in society at large, there is a move away from fragmentation towards purposive leadership and justified priorities. Meanwhile, the Schools Council lies becalmed in troubled seas, hauling down one set of sails and feverishly rigging up another. But it remains to be seen whether it will be able to design and install a rudder.

This is plainly a crucial time for education and curriculum. Centralism is in the air, and to some extent on paper. And yet: the common curriculum is not, and cannot be, a centralist idea. This paradox lies at the heart of the common curriculum. For it has to be about the process of selecting and transforming the culture, and presenting this in a meaningful, motivating way to all pupils: and this cannot be done by government fiat. It can only be done by the sensitive, committed mediation of teachers in individual schools. It rests, as we have seen, on skills in interpreting the culture, skills in human management, and skills at the teacher-pupil interface. It has nothing to do with lists and prescriptions, and everything to do with the school as an adaptive, organic system with a life of its own.

On the face of it, then, our decentralised system is just what is needed to make a common curriculum work. And it is safe to assume that no career politician seriously believes that legislated central direction is acceptable or desirable. The danger is that a failure to understand what the common curriculum really implies will lead to bungled decisions and a lack of finesse at a time when delicacy is all. The essential problem is to determine the degree of intervention which will spark off the process of regeneration, and yet bring strength and purpose to schools. What, in other words, is the right central gesture which will reinforce the periphery? How can political decisions with an unmistakably centralist look about them be framed so as to reinforce the decentralised system on which success depends?

National strategies

We are talking about national education policy, and it is clear that we need to have one: a policy, that is, which goes beyond the mechanics of reorganisation to argue how the quality of education in the reorganised schools can be improved. Better teachers certainly help, and recent decisions regarding college entry requirements and a growing

169

DES interest in in-service training reflect this aspect of policy making. But good teachers do not guarantee a good curriculum, and it is in the area of curriculum policy that action must be taken. Developments like the APU and the Green Paper are tacit acknowledgments of this.

Some framework of national guidelines is a tempting option. In theory, it would not only be a way of activating the curriculum, but also of leading it in desired directions. The difficulty is to see how it can be done in a form which would be both politically and educationally acceptable. To some extent, these come to the same thing: if it is politically acceptable it will be generalised enough to allow power sharing on the lines already discussed, and it would therefore not be so constricting as to inhibit school-based development in a variety of interpretative styles. Too feeble an initiative, though, would present no political difficulties but might not be sufficient to provoke coherent curriculum planning. This seems to be the position at present, more or less; the DES and HMI are making new and louder noises, and the presumption is evidently that in due course, LEAs and schools will dance to this tune. Perhaps this will come about: but it hardly helps that the melody is so poorly articulated.

There is certainly a possible role for the Schools Council here. A working party representing its contributory interests of DES, LEAs and teachers would seem the natural body to draw up guidelines. But Manzer concluded in 1970 that the council 'may be regarded as an assertion of orthodoxy and, quite possibly, an opportunity lost', and Corbett (1975) goes further:

> No one is particularly helped by believing that the Schools Council, as it exists, can provide an effective base for innovation and the propagation of pluralist values. Those who want innovation and diversity ought, it seems to me, to be putting some of the funds in rival concerns.

It is, though, a widely accepted view that despite its earlier misgivings, the DES has encouraged the Secretary of State to give the council a new lease of life under its new constitution, simply because there is no other body in sight which might conceivably carry out tasks of this kind: if it did not exist, it would have to be invented. Even so, the comment of Lord Eccles (quoted in Devlin and Warnock, 1977) on the Schools Council still has the ring of truth:

> It has all the faults of a body of people onto which people are put because they represented somebody or other. You cannot get policy made by people who are always looking over their shoulders to see what the people they represent would think.

And it is significant that the 1978 White Paper on the single system of examining at 16-plus gives the central co-ordinating role not to the Schools Council, but to a separate committee. This strong central body will reflect user interests as well as the schools, and could have a powerful backwash influence on the school curriculum. It has the important political task of sustaining confidence in the new system, and the implication appears to be that a task of this delicacy is beyond the capability of the council.

The problem in laying down national guidelines for the curriculum is every bit as tricky, and by no means as easy as it looks. It calls for exactly the kind of sure-footedness which the council has proved to be so woefully short of — witness working paper No. 53 on the whole curriculum or its numerous attempts to reform the sixth form curriculum. For national guidelines cannot just be bald statements like 'all pupils should be offered scientific experience'. This aim would be met by the present multiple-choice schemes, which simply offer a ragbag of separate science subjects. This is no way to ensure that pupils are initiated into scientific understanding — the need is to teach science as science to all pupils, so that the unifying concepts and methods are challenged and understood. But writing down lists of these is not much help either: it is no way of ensuring that pupils actually learn these things. The guidelines must indicate desirable outcomes rather than areas of content, and do so with enough specificity to make it all worthwhile, but avoiding the detail which cramps and confines. They must offer, too, enough of a rationale to make sense of the scheme and illumine process as well as product, yet not in such a way as to pre-empt the school's need to establish an underpinning rationale in its community context.

On the evidence of *Curriculum 11–16* and the Green

Paper, this is a task which neither the Inspectorate nor the DES could carry off successfully. But without clearer guidelines schools may flounder in a sea of good intentions. Some schools, for example, have reacted to the Green Paper and the current debate by introducing a compulsory 'general studies' component into their fourth and fifth year cores of English, maths and physical education. This is an amalgam of religious, moral and health education with current affairs and careers: one school describes it as 'certain important areas of study about life in general'. This kind of approach is likely to go the same way as sixth form general studies. It has no curriculum unity, constrains the working of core-plus-options systems by reducing the size of the option element, and seems to pupils a pointless appendage with no relevance to the examination goals which loom large in the bulk of curriculum time. It is exactly the wrong way to go about broadening the curriculum: by adding unrelated blobs of content rather than working from first principles to make these experiences part of a planned whole.

One can see, though, that such an approach might be sufficient to enable pupils at 15-plus to pass APU tests in ethical or political awareness — or, rather, to allow a school to assure its governors and LEA officials that its curriculum took account of the whole range of APU tests. In this way the APU tests can themselves act as curriculum guidelines. But instead of lifting a school's horizons and extending the creativity of the staff, they can inhibit large-scale change. Their effect might be simply to promote cheap-jack improvisations cobbled together from the odds and ends of the school's curriculum backyard. And all this would happen in the name of improved standards.

Another development which could have the effect of imposing limits on a school's curriculum activity is the Schools Council's scheme for a common system of examination at 16-plus, now adopted in the 1978 White Paper after the deliberations of the Waddell Committee. The intention is wholly admirable: to replace the present divisive system of O-level and CSE with a single system that will avoid the need for overt division by reason of examination, although abler pupils in some subjects will take additional papers. The trouble is that it is one thing to devise a neutral examination system: quite another for a school to adopt a neutral curriculum policy. Schools wishing to stream will still find plenty of reasons for doing so.

A more serious problem, though, is that the new system may − at least in the short term − lack the diversity which has come about, in an *ad hoc* fashion, under the present divided system. The existence of the CSE boards has encouraged Mode-3 (school-based) styles of examining, and led to the development of interrelated subject courses in some cases. The O-level boards have responded by adopting, and often improving, these initiatives: I know, for example, of a school which has seen its CSE Mode 3 examination in social studies lead directly to a substantially similar mode 1 O-level in this subject. And if necessary, schools have been able to run parallel Mode-3 O-level and CSE examinations in, for example, English, history and geography as part of an interrelated area of study. Thus innovating schools have been able to bend the system to their advantage, and put the curriculum first.

It is by no means certain that the new GCSE examining boards will show this degree of flexibility. They will cover much bigger areas, and might well take on a monolithic aspect. It is doubtful, after all, if either the CSE or the O-level boards would be as accommodating as has been the case over the last decade or so, were it not for each other's existence. Although an element of inter-board choice is retained, the facility to introduce a Mode 3 proposal relatively painlessly is just as important. And the difficulty here is essentially political: if the new GCSE examinations are to be credible to users, they cannot afford to look like a soft option. There is already a tacit suggestion that the poor acceptability of CSE is in part a reason for the new system. The danger is that in seeking to prove that CSE can be 'toughened up' by riding, as it were, on the back of GCE O-level, the opportunities for teacher involvement at the level of school planning (rather than mere bureaucratic participation in the board's administrative structures) will be greatly lessened.

The GCSE proposals are the right idea, but at the wrong time. When the Schools Council first embraced them in

1970, its view of the curriculum as a collection of subjects was unchallenged, and few schools had brought about profitable interactions between GCE and CSE boards by putting O-level and CSE in double harness so as to facilitate school-based development. Given this limited perspective, it made sense to seek to unify each subject examination under, as it were, a single set of starter's orders. But the position has now changed in both respects. Not only has curriculum thinking moved towards a common curriculum, with its implications of interrelations between subjects; the last eight years have also seen a vigorous growth of mode 1 examinations at both O-level and CSE in response to the needs of schools – and some of these are in interrelated areas, like environmental and social studies. Little wonder, then, that a puzzled headmaster can write (Duffy, 1978) of the mismatch between the aspirations of *Curriculum 11–16*, and the reality of the proposed common GCSE system of examining:

> The assumption [of the GCSE proposals] is that the curriculum in the schools of today and tomorrow can be adequately described in terms of subjects. . . . The HMIs pleaded for . . . a curriculum capable of responding to the changing needs of a pluralist society. . . . By implication they pleaded for an examination system capable of assessing this curriculum. . . . The proposed new system may be new but its assumptions and its framework are certainly not . . .

The irony is that, with all its drawbacks, the present O-level/CSE system makes it perfectly possible, as I know from my own experience, to mount and examine a common curriculum on the lines now advocated in *Curriculum 11–16*. Eventually, when the new system has settled down, it may well be possible to make an even better fit between curriculum and examination. But until then, it seems likely that the political birth-pangs of the new system will make life that much harder for schools anxious to implement whole-curriculum planning with the school as its focus.

What it comes down to is the need to see the council's scheme not merely as yet another piecemeal improvement, but part of a consistent policy with the whole curriculum at its centre. So we come back to the question of whether the revamped council is capable of a quite fundamental personality change, so that it can define coherent policy and, as Owen put it in the passage quoted earlier, 'rejustify itself in terms of the Green Paper'. The new governing structure may prove to be as limiting as the old. The review body has done the best anyone could, but it cannot change the council's genetic make-up, and the pattern of committees is not exactly streamlined. For consider: the new tier of convocation will have 56 members; the finance and priorities committee 28; the professional committee 37; the primary curriculum committee 20; the secondary curriculum committee 24; and the examinations committee 32. This makes the remarkable total of 197 people as part of the decision-making structure. The fact that some of them will sit on more than one body may reassure some; others may find it a little unnerving.

Let us put this in perspective by considering the Australian Curriculum Development Centre, which was formally established by an Act of the Australian Parliament in 1975. Its governing council has 15 members, including a part-time chairman and permanent full-time director. The Australian Education Council (a government body corresponding roughly to our former Association of Education Committees, but without any direct English equivalent) has three nominees, and other interests represented are the Schools Commission, the Education Research and Development Committee, the Independent Schools, the Australian Teachers' Federation (one nominee), the Commonwealth Department of Education, the Council of State School Organisations, the Catholic Education System, and Teacher Education Institutions. The Centre's fundamental aim is to 'foster curriculum and materials development from pre-school to post-secondary levels' (Curriculum Development Centre 1977) and it does not 'take those overall policy and implementation decisions which are appropriate to the State and Federal Departments of Education, the Schools Commission, the schools themselves and the wider community'.

The purpose of the CDC is thus very close to that of the Schools Council, and it works broadly within the same

175

limitations. But its decisions are guided by 15 people rather than 200, and its permanent directorate makes it possible for clear lines of policy to be established. Compare, for example, the Schools Council's list of projects it has backed – an assortment of titles, mainly subject-based and ability-specific, and often overlapping – with the CDC's identification of three major project categories: *research projects*, directed towards establishing priorities for future curriculum development work; *development projects*, which usually result in published resources or 'new approaches to teacher-pupil interaction'; and *seed projects*, which might be feasibility studies for larger-scale projects, or lead to such projects. Furthermore, there is

> a major emphasis on school-based approaches including the support required to make the school an effective agent of curriculum and cultural renewal. . . . There can be no doubt about the need to provide various kinds of support and guidance if teachers are to cope with the new requirements.

It would be naïve to suggest that the Schools Council's operations have been wholly misconceived, or that the CDC is incapable of error. But it is remarkable that two bodies with roughly the same function in life should work in such very different ways, and regard curriculum development in such very different terms. Both are really interventionist agencies: but while the CDC seems at least to have taken a professional view of the business, the Schools Council seems to have fumbled many of its opportunities, and in some important ways to be out of touch with schools. It could be of immense help in promoting curriculum re-generation: under a permanent secretariat it may find its voice.

So the future for a framework of national guidelines must be seen as uncertain. The best we can hope for is a broader perception of mass secondary education, operating at two levels. The more abstract level would derive from a recognition that the economic future may be rather different from that assumed in the Green Paper: in essence, the model of the 1960s mixed economy, maintaining full employment and sufficient growth to expand the public sector. There is a view now that unemployment may be structural and not transitory, and the rapid development of micro-processors is beginning to make all those predictions of an automated future – a prophetic theme since the 1950s, as we have noted – look like coming true.

In either case, the appropriate curriculum for society is the one which is right for the individual – a curriculum which initiates pupils into key aspects of the culture. But with the first scenario, a degree of imagination is needed to see that instrumental aims are better served by a curriculum which gives pupils the autonomy to make sense of the world and go on learning, than one which is 'work-oriented' and is geared, for most pupils at any rate, to practical, 'outward-looking' courses. There will be glib talk of 'a smooth transition from school to work', and the remoteness of Oxbridge from the world of technology tends to be thrown into the argument for good measure. The traditional grammar school curriculum assuredly reflects this deep-rooted prejudice against the world of making and doing: but that is precisely why a broad, common curriculum is needed. The trouble is that in political terms, this argument can easily be muddled up with the popular belief that nothing can possibly be wrong with the grammar school curriculum: and so we lurch from one misunderstanding to another.

With the second scenario, the argument for a common curriculum is more accessible. Work is not something that all must aspire to, and society exists to create: there is simply not enough work to go round. It follows that we must begin to talk about a smooth transition from school to the world of culture, rather than of work: the world of leisure, books, conversation and sport, and a world where personal fulfilment is not merely a matter of producing and consuming wealth. The point has been made, for instance, in a speech by Professor Stonier (reported in *The Times Educational Supplement*, 6.1.78):

The primary function of education in the future should not be to teach a student how to make a living but how to live. As Western countries moved more and more into automation, fewer workers would be needed. . . . This did not mean Britain would become poorer because it was a myth that wealth was only created by expanding manufacturing industry. Knowledge creates wealth as well. . . . What is shaping up is a . . . productive system which produces as much wealth using only 10 per cent of the labour force. This leaves 90 per cent to do what human beings really like best, which is to take care of one another in education, health and social services. . . .

The purpose of compulsory schooling has, of course, always been to teach a student how to live: but the forced retreat from the work ethic makes this an easier political concept to grasp. It will be a painful process for many vested interests, but it ought to help put school in the right perspective.

The second level of perception is, again, an aspect of a cultural-synthesis common curriculum which becomes more accessible when there is less opportunity for confused thinking about school and work. It is the recognition that education is neither a seamless garment of knowledge nor a collection of separately-boxed subjects, but a process of 'unpacking' cultural experiences which makes use of conceptual structures to guide the pupil over a map of the culture. The first perception is about schooling: the second is about teaching. The teacher is valuable not because he possesses an encashable body of knowledge, but because of the way he uses his whole store of understanding and experience to allow the pupil to share his cultural vision, and so to construct his own. It is a dynamic rather than a static view, and implies that teachers, like pupils, must go on learning.

Regional strategies

It is perhaps this second kind of perception which will be important in determining initiatives at the regional level. For the need here is to move from generalisations about the shape of the whole curriculum to practical solutions in the school and the support these imply for schools and teachers. Good relations between national agencies, like the DES and

Schools Council, and the local authorities will be essential if the necessary expansion of the infrastructure is to be truly effective. As Owen (1977) has written:

> This is a time when those who should be responsible for the improvement of curriculum are separated from each other. White Papers on public expenditure give no protection to teacher improvement other than words. We wander around in a limbo of argument about earmarking parts of the rate-support grant for in-service training and induction.

Without a clearer conception of curriculum policy, there may be further confusion before co-operation. It would certainly be a straightforward step for the Schools Council to link up more closely with LEAs in extending its field operations. One regional information centre has been operating since 1973, in Newcastle. The idea came from the Newcastle LEA, and was a joint venture, using a council grant and LEA premises. But its success has led to no others. What is really needed is a major expansion of the field service to provide through local centres not only information, but also support for local school-based projects using council funds. And instead of the short-term field officer secondments, the council needs a permanent staff with its own career structure, corresponding to a devolution of power from the centre into the regions where new curriculum schemes are actually to be implemented. This kind of operation has been foreseen by Eraut (1972):

> There would seem to be a need for developing centres . . . in which the activities of projects would be studied along with problems encountered by schools . . . after the projects had ended; and in which potential members of curriculum development teams could receive some training. These centres could also provide consultancy help to projects of a more substantial nature than the occasional visit . . . .

There seems no reason why a centre of this kind should not be based at a teachers' centre: it would be a palpable example of Schools Council-LEA links. There is much to be said for tying teachers' centres more explicitly to substantive curriculum development in their area.

But this would be only part of what is needed. Within local authorities, there is a need for applied research and development units which should be seen as a way of linking the LEA more closely with the work of schools. An adviser can tell an education officer or committee member which schools have courses in environmental studies; but if LEAs are to play a part in facilitating whole-curriculum change, there is a case for a developmental arm which would be equipped to discuss the shape of the curriculum in an extensive yet informal way with heads and staff in schools, and would help both to initiate change and to sustain it. Such a unit should be kept free of the routine bureaucracy and administration which cannot be separated from the advisory service. It need have no more than three or four members in an average county authority, and two of these might well be seconded heads with a track record of sound innovation. It would enter schools only at the request of head and staff, and would offer a service of appraisal and facilitation rather than consultancy. It is difficult to see how effective consultancy work in schools can be undertaken by direct LEA employees, but the separation of this *curriculum unit* from the advisory service would reduce its 'Janus' aspect sufficiently to make these system-based developmental studies perfectly possible. It should report direct to the chief education officer rather than the chief adviser, and advisory policies for INSET and school support services would then be framed in the light of these studies and, of course, the information available to the advisory service.

The concept of the curriculum unit would be unpopular with officers and advisers alike. But it would be a success with schools if it meant that they could sense a genuine engagement between their interpretation of the whole curriculum and the policies and intentions of the authority. The use of seconded heads to staff the unit would enhance this engagement, partly by involving doers rather than talkers — it is an uncomfortable distinction, but one which schools will readily make — and partly by showing that it is not just another expansion of those who add to the cost of education but seem too remote from teaching to those who have to get on with it. An incidental benefit is that it would offer lively heads a chance to expand their horizons to the benefit of the authority – and the lack of a career structure for heads is a serious weakness at present, which would be eased if the education service could be more dynamically involved with school-based development. The curriculum unit would also be a way of linking school-based development to research ideas, for its permanent staff would have – unlike advisers – the time to maintain their knowledge of curriculum theory. It would also help system-based developments in schools to retain a broad alignment with local interpretations of national policies. And it would link closely with the field services of the Schools Council and the local knowledge acquired by teachers' centre wardens. The work of Rudduck quoted earlier has brought out the uneven nature of the relationship between wardens and advisers. The unit would, in short, be a practical expression of a general need to link things together better. The point has been made by Havelock (1971):

> The pieces of the educational revolution are lying around unassembled; we need to build systems that would link the research world and the practice world to each other on a continuous basis for their mutual gain.

Local strategies

We have now arrived at the point where we must consider strategies that lie at the level of the school. We have suggested some ways in which schools might be better linked to national and regional agencies, but there is much to be done that would assist the innovating school with the management of change. Some of these have already arisen: local co-operatives for the production of materials, for example, and the general responsibility of LEA advisory services for the provision and co-ordination of course-based INSET, making use of available facilities in higher education institutions not only to harness their in-house courses but also to provide courses tailor-made to service the strategies fostered by the LEA curriculum unit.

But more specialised services will be needed. An example

of the kind of intervention that will benefit the innovating school is the Avon Resources for Learning Development Unit, which runs an experimental classroom to help local teachers in practical decision-making, and also offers a consultancy service to innovating schools (Waterhouse, 1977b):

> The unit staff members are going into schools as partners to the teaching staff. . . . Decisions are made about objectives, about classes, rooms, resources and the extent of the involvement of each of the partners. . . . Sometimes the consultants take over entirely for a few weeks, leaving the teachers with the opportunity to observe, reflect and discuss. . . . Results so far suggest that the strategy pays off, that teachers find the whole operation stimulating . . . .

This unit has a particular interest in independent learning. There is a case for extending this kind of development to other techniques which have a vital part to play in developing an effective common curriculum: forms of integration between subject areas, non-streaming and team teaching are all obvious candidates. There is, of course, a danger in seeing these as separate, almost competing areas: far better for LEAs to think in terms not of units, but of an integrated support service which might encourage a local bias and so offer a complete county-wide service.

This amounts to an INSET provision which has its base outside the school, but exists solely to further school-based curriculum development, The other need is for consultancy help which is based in the school itself, and which has been discussed in the previous chapter. It could take a number of forms, and might be associated with the design, implementation or evaluation stages of whole-curriculum planning. It might, as in the previous example, be associated with a local support service; or it might be linked with a national project which, like the Schools Council Geography 14–18 Project, draws its strength from school roots. This is assuredly the kind of national project which makes sense in the context of school-based change, and it is clear that initiatives of this kind will be needed. The CDC has, for example, launched the Australian Science Education Project and the Social Education Materials Project, and has recently set up a new programme for Core Curriculum and Values Education. In the past, most Schools Council projects have lacked the breadth and scope to make them a useful part of a school-based common curriculum: either through a narrowness of definition by ability-group or subject, or by a centre-periphery alignment which leaves little room for teachers' own cultural interpretations. Whether or not the council frames a coherent policy for the whole curriculum, it is to be hoped that its future project ventures will at least reflect a wider context. And ideally, the field consultancy services available to schools would be an aspect of the work of new regional Schools Council centres.

Other consultancy teams might come from independent agencies or from professional centres. The key quality is credibility, and this implies consultants with first-hand knowledge of the tasks and responsibilities faced by schools involved in whole-curriculum change. The main aim should be to recruit these people – as the Keele project co-ordinators were recruited – from schools. There is much talk of the need for staff development in schools, but little sign that LEAs have begun to see the need to foster career development. This is particularly important for senior management in schools, and the demand in the future for consultants and INSET trainers means that LEAs should see talent-spotting of this kind as too important to leave to chance. It is remarkable that teachers' organisations have paid so little attention to this aspect of professionalism.

Ideally, we need more fluent mechanisms for people to move between schools and academic centres. The theoretical perspective that is derived from a research discipline can be of the first importance, but it must be informed by practical interpretation. For example, in discussing Bernstein's well-known (1971) distinction between collected and integrated curricula, Jenkins and Shipman (1976) comment that:

The contrasts outlined by Bernstein seemed too dramatic in the context of these schools. Social scientists are probably too prone to see schools as organisations with

183

rigid structures similar to those found in hospitals, fac-
tories, prisons or concentration camps, where most work
on organisations has been carried out.

Consultancy teams need to include not social scientists or
philosophers or psychologists as such, but rather as disciplines represented by the varied experience and insight of the
consultants. And by the same token, consultants are, as in
Waterhouse's example, people who can work and identify
with teachers. For a time, their own base may be a professional centre or consultancy service: but as they come
from schools, so will they return to them.

Expanding the infrastructure of education is a necessity,
and I have suggested a number of ways in which this might
be done. But unless the expansion process is geared at every
step to the real needs of schools, we might well end up
with the kind of over-elaborated structure which has pro-
liferated within the National Health Service. While regenerating the curriculum is a matter of national concern and,
indeed, of national policy, it has its roots in the creative
processes of teachers in schools. Too much bureaucratic
planning will bring it in conflict with the individualism on
which, as Reynolds and Skilbeck (1976) observe, success
depends:

> School-based curriculum development is in line with
> those movements in contemporary culture which give
> prominence to activism by small groups, the questioning
> of traditional hierarchies, and the substitution of the
> critical processes of inquiry and valuation for those of
> assimilation and value acceptance.

There are several reasons why we could see the kind of over-
planning which would be just as objectionable and un-
productive as the present under-planning. One is the lack of
any real education policy in either of the main political
parties; another is the irresolution of the Schools Council;
and another is the prospect that in-service education and
training could be a bonanza for a great many individuals
and institutions. A sizeable sum of money will be up for
grabs as the INSET rhetoric is turned into reality, and already
a number of bodies are edging forward with pilot schemes

for this and that. The worrying thing is that INSET, like evaluation, is an activity which can grow fat at the expense of schools, and ostensibly with the intention of helping them: yet at the end of the day, neither may have done much good. Indeed, in the case of evaluation, some American experiences suggest that it can be positively harmful.

This is not meant to be an unduly cynical view: it certainly need not turn out like this. But unless there is a wider perception of the school-based nature of curriculum development and of coherent planning at national and regional levels, then we could see a flurry of course-based and school-based activity which would bring gainful employment to armies of pure researchers, projecteers and academics, but lead to very little significant change in the quality of education that pupils actually receive.

And there is still some way to go. What Wells wrote seventy years ago in *The New Machiavelli* still sounds like a challenge:

> If humanity cannot develop an education far beyond anything that it now provides, if it cannot, collectively, invent devices and solve problems on a much richer and broader scale than it does at the present time, it cannot hope to achieve any very much finer order or any more general happiness than it now enjoys.

One unsolved problem is that of extending to every pupil an understanding of his cultural inheritance; and the need to do so seems clearer now than ever. But the solution is in the realm of the possible, and enough is known about it to indicate how we could extend it to our schools. It is worth taking the trouble to develop the strategies for innovation and regeneration that could bring this about.

Bibliography

Bailey, C. (1975), 'Neutrality and rationality in teaching', in D. Bridges and P. Scrimshaw (ed.), *Values and Authority in Schools*, Hodder & Stoughton.

Bailey, C. (1978), 'A strange debate: some comments on the Green Paper', *Cambridge Journal of Education*, Lent.

Barnes, D., Britten, J. and Rosen, H. (1969), *Language, the Learner and the School*, Penguin Books.

Baxter, B. (1972), 'Discipline', *ROSLA Book 3*, BBC Publications.

Becher, R.A. and Maclure, S. (1978), *The Politics of Curriculum Change*, Hutchinson.

Bernbaum, G. (1973), 'Countesthorpe College', *Case Studies of Educational Innovation III*, CERI/OECD, Paris.

Bernstein, B. (1971), *Class, Codes and Control I*, Routledge & Kegan Paul.

Bloom, B. (ed.) (1956), *Taxonomy of Educational Objectives*, Longman.

Bolam, R. (1974), *Planned Educational Change: Theory and Practice*, University of Bristol.

Bolam, R. (1977), 'Innovation and the problem-solving school', in E. King (ed.), *Reorganising Education: Management and Participation for Change*, Sage Publications.

Bolam, R., Smith, G. and Canter, H. (1976), *Local Education Authority Advisers and Educational Innovation*, University of Bristol.

Booker, C. (1969), *The Neophiliacs*, Collins.

Boydell, D. (1977), 'Researching the informal junior classroom', in C. Richards (ed.), *New Contexts for Teaching, Learning and Curriculum Studies*, Association for the Study of the Curriculum.

Broudy, H., Smith, B. and Burnett, B. (1965), *Democracy and Excellence in American Secondary Education*, Rand McNally.

Browne, S. (1977), 'Curriculum: an HMI view', *Trends in Education*, 3.

Burstall, C. *et al.* (1974), *Primary French in the Balance*, NFER.

Clark, J. (1971), 'A Scottish viewpoint', *ROSLA Book 2*, BBC Publications.

Clegg, Sir A. (1975), 'A view from the West Riding', in R. Bell and W. Prescott (ed.), *The Schools Council: A Second Look*, Ward Lock Educational.

Comber, L., Foster, A. and Whitfield, R. (1977), 'An analysis of the middle school curriculum', *Research in Middle Schools*, Dept. of Educational Enquiry, Aston University, Birmingham.

Corbett, A. (1975), 'Teachers and the Schools Council', in R. Bell and W. Prescott (ed.), *The Schools Council: A Second Look*, Ward Lock Educational.

Curriculum Development Centre (1977), *Triennial Program 1977–79*, Canberra, Australia.

D'Arcy, P. (1978), 'On whom the toll falls', *The Times Educational Supplement*, 3 February.

Davis, R. (1967), *The Grammar School*, Penguin Books.

Davies, B. (1976), *Social Control and Education*, Methuen.

Dean, J. (1975), 'The role of the local advisory service in the in-service education of teachers', in E. Adams (ed.), *In-Service Education and Teaching Centres*, Pergamon.

Department of Education and Science:
Education in Schools: a Consultative Document (1977), Cmnd 6869, HMSO.
Curriculum 11–16 (1977), Working papers by HMI, DES.
Ten Good Schools (1977), DES HMI series No. 1, HMSO.
Gifted Children in Middle and Comprehensive Secondary Schools (1977), DES HMI series No. 4, HMSO.
A New Partnership for our Schools (1977), HMSO.

Devlin, T. and Warnock, M. (1977), *What Must We Teach?*, Temple Smith.

Duffy, M. (1978), 'The thoughts of HMI', *Guardian*, 17 October.

Eichholz, G. and Rogers, E. (1964), 'Resistance to the adoption of audio-visual aids by elementary school teachers', in M. Miles (ed.), *Innovation in Education*, Teachers' College, Columbia.

Elliott, J. and Adelman, C. (1974), *Innovation in Teaching and Action Research*, University of East Anglia.

Eraut, M. (1972), *In-Service Education for Innovation*, National Council for Educational Technology.

Gibson, R. (1978), 'A slave to limit: the dogmatism of educational research', *Cambridge Journal of Education*, Lent.

187

Gross, N., Giacquinta, J. and Bernstein, M. (1971), *Implementing Organisational Innovations: Analysis of Planned Change*, Harper & Row.

Guba, E. and Clark, O. (1967), 'An examination of potential change roles in education', *Rational Planning in Curriculum and Instruction*, NEA, Washington.

Hamilton, D. (1976), *Curriculum Evaluation*, Open Books.

Havelock, R.G. (1969), *Planning for Innovation through Dissemination and Utilisation of Knowledge*, University of Michigan.

Havelock, R.G. (1971), 'The utilisation of educational research and development', *British Journal of Educational Technology*, 2 (2).

Henderson, E. (1978), 'School-focused INSET: another perspective', mimeo for conference 'Towards a national and local policy for in-service training', Advisory Committee on the Supply and Training of Teachers, 17–19 January.

Hilsum, S. and Strong, C.R. (1978), *The Secondary Teacher's Day*, NFER.

Hirst, P.H. (1965), 'Liberal education and the nature of knowledge', in R. Archambault (ed.), *Philosophical Analysis and Education*, Routledge & Kegan Paul.

Hirst, P.H. (1973), 'Towards a logic of curriculum development', in P. Taylor and J. Walton (ed.), *The Curriculum: Research, Innovation and Change*, Ward Lock Educational.

Hirst, P.H. (1975), 'The forms of knowledge revisited', *Knowledge and the Curriculum*, Routledge & Kegan Paul.

Hirst, P.H. and Peters, R.S. (1970), *The Logic of Education*, Routledge & Kegan Paul.

Holt, M. (1978), *The Common Curriculum*, Routledge & Kegan Paul.

Hoyle, E. (1971), 'The role of the change agent in educational innovation', in J. Walton (ed.), *Curriculum Organisation and Design*, Ward Lock Educational.

Hoyle, E. (1972), *Problems of Curriculum Innovation II*, Course E 283 Unit 17, Open University.

Hoyle, E. (1973), 'Strategies of curriculum change', in R. Watkins (ed.), *In-Service Training: Structure and Content*, Ward Lock Educational.

Hoyle, E. (1975), 'The creativity of the school in Britain', in A. Harris *et al.* (ed.), *Curriculum Innovation*, Croom Helm.

Jackson, P. (1968), *Life in Classrooms*, Holt, Rinehart & Winston.

Jenkins, D. (1976), 'Curriculum evaluation', Course E 203 Units 19–20, Open University.

Jenkins, D. (1977), 'Curriculum evaluation', in C. Richards (ed.),

New Contexts for Teaching, Learning and Curriculum Studies, Association for the Study of the Curriculum.

Jenkins, D. and Shipman, M. (1976), *Curriculum: An Introduction*, Open Books.

Kogan, M. (1972), 'Administrative relationships between the school and outside institutions', 'Creativity of the School' Project, CERI/CS/72.04, OECD, Paris.

Lawton, D. (1970), 'Preparations for changes in the curriculum', in J.W. Tibble (ed.), *The Extra Year*, Routledge & Kegan Paul.

Lawton, D. (1975), *Class, Culture and the Curriculum*, Routledge & Kegan Paul.

Lawton, D. (1977a), 'Curricular reorientation', in E. King (ed.), *Reorganising Education: Management and Participation for Change*, Sage Publications.

Lawton, D. (1977b), 'Curriculum: case for power-sharing', *The Times Educational Supplement*, 17 June.

MacDonald, B. (1973), 'Innovation and incompetence', in D. Hamingson (ed.), *Towards Judgement*, Centre for Applied Research in Education, University of East Anglia.

MacDonald-Ross, M. (1975), 'Behavioural objectives – a critical review', *Management in Education Reader 2*, Ward Lock Educational.

Maclure, S. (1965), *Educational Documents England and Wales*, Chapman & Hall.

Maclure, S. (1968), *Curriculum Innovation in Practice*, HMSO.

McMullen, I. (1968), 'Flexibility for a comprehensive school', *Forum in Education*, Spring.

Manzer, R. (1970), *Teachers and Politics*, Manchester University Press.

Miles, M. (1964), *Innovation in Education*, Columbia University.

Miles, M. (1965), 'Planned change and organisational health: figure and ground', in R. Carlson (ed.), *Change Processes in the Public Schools*, University of Oregon.

Munn Report, *see* Scottish Education Department.

Munro, R. (1977), *Innovation – Success or Failure?*, Hodder & Stoughton.

Nevermann, K. (1974), 'The relationship of the formal organisation of, and informal grouping within, a school to its creativity', working paper for *'Creativity of the School'* Project, CERI/CS/74.26, OECD, Paris.

Nisbet, J. (1973), 'Strengthening the creativity of the school', in *Creativity of the School*, OECD/CERI.

Nisbet, J. (1974), 'Innovation − bandwagon or hearse?' in A. Harris *et al.* (ed.), *Curriculum Innovation* (1975), Croom Helm.

Open University (1976) Course E203:
Case Study 2, *The Sidney Stringer Community School.*
Case Study 5, *Portrait of Countesthorpe College.*

Owen, J. (1973), *The Management of Curriculum Development*, Cambridge University Press.

Owen, J. (1977), 'Schools Council: a beginning, a middle . . . and now?', *The Times Educational Supplement*, 17 June.

Pedley, R. (1964), *The Comprehensive School*, Penguin Books.

Peters, R.S. (1977), *Education and the Education of Teachers*, Routledge & Kegan Paul.

Phenix, P. (1964), *The Realms of Meaning*, McGraw-Hill.

Porter, J. (1975), 'The in-service education of teachers and the colleges of education', in E. Adams (ed.), *In-Service Education and Teaching Centres*, Pergamon.

Pring, R. (1975), 'In defence of authority', in D. Bridges and P. Scrimshaw (ed.), *Values and Authority in Schools*, Hodder & Stoughton.

Pring, R. (1976), *Knowledge and Schooling*, Open Books.

Reynolds, J. (1976), *Portrait of a National Project*, Open University.

Reynolds, J. and Skilbeck, M. (1976), *Culture and the Classroom*, Open Books.

Richardson, E. (1975), *Authority and Organisation in the Secondary School*, Macmillan.

Rudduck, J. (1976), *Dissemination of Innovation: The Humanities Curriculum Project*, Evans/Methuen.

Rudduck, J. (1978), 'School-based curriculum development and external agencies', mimeo for conference on the common curriculum, Cambridge Institute of Education, 21–24 September.

Rudduck, J. and Kelly, P. (1976), *The Dissemination of Curriculum Development*, Council of Europe.

Schon, D. (1971), *Beyond the Stable State*, Penguin Books.

Schwab, J.J. (1969), 'The practical: a language for curriculum', *School Review*, November.

Scottish Education Department: *The Structure of the Curriculum in the Third and Fourth Years of the Scottish Secondary School* (The Munn Report) (1977), HMSO.

Shipman, M. (1974), *Inside a Curriculum Project*, Methuen.

Skilbeck, M. (1971), 'Strategies of curriculum change', in J. Walton (ed.), *Curriculum Organisation and Design*, Ward Lock Educational.

Skilbeck, M. (1972), 'Administrative decisions and cultural values', *Journal of Educational Administration*, Vol. X, No. 2.

Skilbeck, M. (1975), 'School-based curriculum development and the task of in-service education', in E. Adams (ed.), *In-Service Education and Teaching Centres*, Pergamon.

Skilbeck, M. (1976a), *Culture, Ideology and Knowledge*, Course E 203, Open University.

Skilbeck, M. (1976b), 'Basic questions in curriculum', *The Scope of Curriculum Study*, Course E 203, Open University.

Skilbeck, M. (1976c), 'The curriculum development process: a model for school use', in H. McMahon (ed.), *Styles of Curriculum Development*, Course E 203, Open University.

Snape, P. (1972), 'Changing management ideas and the timetable', in J. Walton (ed.), *The Secondary School Timetable*, Ward Lock Educational.

Sockett, H. (1976), 'Approaches to curriculum planning', *Rationality and Artistry*, Course E 203, Open University.

Stake, R. (1967), 'The countenance of educational evaluation', *Teachers' College Record*, 68, 523–40.

Stenhouse, L. (1975), *An Introduction to Curriculum Development*, Heinemann.

Stephens, J. (1975), 'Some current issues for teacher in-service education', in E. Adams (ed.), *In-Service Education and Teachers' Centres*, Pergamon.

Taylor, L.C. (1972), 'Individual learning', in *ROSLA Book 4*, BBC Publications.

Taylor, W. (1977), 'Teachers and the continuous reorientation of education', in E. King (ed.), *Reorganising Education: Management and Participation for Change*, Sage Publications.

Thornbury, R. (1973) (ed.), *Teachers' Centres*, Darton, Longman & Todd.

Townsend, H. (1970), 'The in-service training of teachers in primary and secondary schools', in *DES Statistics of Education No. 2*, HMSO.

Vickers, G. (1973), *Making Institutions Work*, Associated Business Programmes.

Walker, R. (1977), 'Classroom Research', in C. Richards (ed.), *New Contexts for Teaching, Learning and Curriculum Studies*, Association for the Study of the Curriculum.

Walker, R. and Adelman, C. (1975), *A Guide to Classroom Observation*, Methuen.

Warnock, M. (1977), *Schools of Thought*, Faber.

Waterhouse, P. (1977a), 'Staff development in two contexts', in C. Richards (ed.), *New Contexts for Teaching, Learning and Curriculum Studies*, Association for the Study of the Curriculum.

Waterhouse, P. (1977b), 'Managing performance', *The Times Educational Supplement*, 7 January.

Waterhouse, P. (1978), *A Handbook of Classroom Management for Independent Learning*, Resources for Learning Development Unit, Bristol.

White, J. (1972), 'Creativity in education: a philosophical analysis', in R. Dearden *et al.* (ed.), *Education and the Development of Reason*, Routledge & Kegan Paul.

Whitehead, A. (1962), *The Aims of Education*, Benn.

Wolfe, T. (1976), 'The painted word', in *Harpers and Queen*, February.

Index